MW00329667

AGAINST the KLAN

MEDIA AND PUBLIC AFFAIRS

Robert Mann, Series Editor

Highway 36 in St. Tammany Parish south of Bogalusa, Louisiana.

AGAINST
the KLAN

**A NEWSPAPER PUBLISHER
IN SOUTH LOUISIANA
DURING THE 1960S**

LOU MAJOR
Foreword by STANLEY NELSON

LOUISIANA STATE UNIVERSITY PRESS

BATON ROUGE

Published by Louisiana State University Press
www.lsupress.org

Direct quotations, letters to the editor, and news stories appear herein courtesy of the *Bogalusa Daily News*. Photographs courtesy of the *Bogalusa Daily News* unless otherwise indicated. Frontispiece photograph courtesy of Lou Major Jr.

Designer: Barbara Neely Bourgoyne
Typeface: Whitman

Jacket photograph courtesy The Long Civil Rights Movement Collection: Photographs from the Ronnie Moore Papers, 1964–1972; Amistad Research Center; New Orleans, Louisiana

Library of Congress Cataloging-in-Publication Data
Names: Major, Lou, 1931–2012, author. | Nelson, Stanley, 1955 September 18– writer of foreword.
Title: Against the Klan : a newspaper publisher in South Louisiana during the 1960s / Lou Major ; foreword by Stanley Nelson.
Description: Baton Rouge : Louisiana State University Press, 2021. | Series: Media and public affairs
Identifiers: LCCN 2020042737 (print) | LCCN 2020042738 (ebook) | ISBN 978-0-8071-7492-0 (cloth) | ISBN 978-0-8071-7540-8 (pdf) | ISBN 978-0-8071-7541-5 (epub)
Subjects: LCSH: Major, Lou, 1931–2012. | Journalists—Louisiana—Biography. | Publishers and publishing—Louisiana—Bogalusa—Biography. | Newspaper publishing—Louisiana—Bogalusa—History—20th century. | Daily news (Bogalusa, La.)—History—20th century. | Ku Klux Klan (1915–)—Louisiana—Bogalusa—Press coverage. | Civil rights movements—Louisiana—Bogalusa—Press coverage. | Bogalusa (La.)—Race relations—Press coverage.
Classification: LCC PN4874.M196 A3 2021 (print) | LCC PN4874.M196 (ebook) | DDC 070.92 [B]—dc23
LC record available at https://lccn.loc.gov/2020042737
LC ebook record available at https://lccn.loc.gov/2020042738

Dedicated to Peggy Major

*My loving wife, lifelong partner and companion,
and steadfast supporter*

CONTENTS

FOREWORD

In 1965, a panel of federal judges in New Orleans determined that seg-regation in Washington Parish and its largest town, Bogalusa, was prac-ticed from "cradle to coffin," a way of life the local Original Knights of the Ku Klux Klan was determined to maintain during the Civil Rights Era. This was not a news flash for Lou Major, editor and publisher of the *Bogalusa Daily News*. A decade earlier, he had joined the newspaper as a cub reporter after earning a journalism degree from Louisiana State University. Soon afterward, while reporting the police beat, he made an error: In his story he mistakenly identified a man booked into jail as "N" for "Negro." Once the paper hit the streets, the man, who was white, stormed into the newsroom. He was not furious that his alleged crime—selling lewd and lascivious literature—had been printed for the world to see. No, he was beside himself that he had been identified as an "N," a designation he felt was akin to calling him "a damned nigger." When he threatened to sue the paper, the publisher at the time real-ized the man might well be victorious before a Bogalusa judge or jury. To avoid that, the paper settled, buying the irate racist a new suit and writing him a check for 75 dollars. Having listened as the man berated his editor and publisher, Major feared he would be fired. Instead, his boss warned him "this would be a lesson for me in the future." At that moment, Major realized that the racial divide in Bogalusa was greater than in any place he had ever been and it would be his job years later to guide the newspaper through a period in the 1960s when the town seemed headed for a race war.

In *Against the Klan: A Newspaper Publisher in South Louisiana during the 1960s,* Major provides an eyewitness account of the Klan's battle against civil rights in Bogalusa as well as the Klan's war against him and his newspaper. Few in Louisiana are aware today that Bogalusa once was considered the most racist town in the United States. Despite that, leaders of some of the largest civil rights organizations in the country, particularly the Congress of Racial Equality (CORE), joined courageous local Black activists on the streets to demand their rights. These demands were met head-on by one of the most violent Klan groups in the country that, along with white segregationists, attacked marchers, threatened whites who showed any moderate views on race, and organized politically to take control of Washington Parish. They came close, helping to elect segregationist leader Judge John Rarick of St. Francisville as Sixth District Congressman of Louisiana and ousting the moderate incumbent Jimmie Morrison of Hammond. The Klan also supported the establishment of a rival paper to compete with the *Daily News* and used it as a tool to help elect Rarick. To get rid of this competition, Major made a business decision and purchased the paper from a third party for less than one thousand dollars.

Unlike most newspaper publishers throughout the South and Louisiana, Major stood up to the KKK, criticized Klansmen for their violence and for terrifying the community. He had no fear even though he knew the Klan bloodied and killed its opposition. He supported the rule of law, knowing and supporting the fact that the Civil Rights Act of 1964 and the Voting Rights Act of 1965 meant the road to integration would lead to the doors of churches, schools, and public buildings and facilities. It also meant that with the power to vote, Blacks would now have a voice and would be elected to public office. So great would be the local Klan's battle to preserve white supremacy that in June 1965 a KKK wrecking crew targeted the parish's first two Black deputies hired by the white sheriff. In a drive-by shooting, Klansmen killed one deputy and severely injured the other. The horrible story unfolded in the pages of the *Daily News.* Yet to this day, the case has never been solved.

While other newspapers provided only venomous coverage of civil rights activities, Major's reporting was mostly fair and informative, although he acknowledges in his memoir that he could have done more and he could have done better. Yet at a time when the country was seemingly at war over race, Major dared do what few white publishers did anywhere in the South, let alone in Louisiana: He editorialized against the Klan. In a number of stories in early 1964, he reported that about one hundred and fifty crosses had been burned in southeastern Louisiana, including eight in Bogalusa. "We wonder whether these nightriders think of the feelings of children and wives in homes where they planted their dirty flaming crosses," he wrote in an editorial. "Obviously, they are people without conscience, bent only on spreading fear." This was an insulting and threatening stance to Klansmen who soon targeted Major. The Klan used its pamphlet, "The Midnight Mail," to smear Major and other town and state leaders who expressed a willingness to obey the federal mandate for integration. The Klan publication, Major writes, was a single sheet of "racial hatred rolled up and bound by a small rubber band."

The Klan also waged an economic boycott against the *Daily News* and other local leaders who worked to resolve racial differences. One of the leaders of this effort was a hostile racist and leader of the Bogalusa Klan who operated a service station near the newspaper office. Major's paper boxes were stolen. Over a two-month period, he lost 1,000 white subscribers but was encouraged as he received messages of support from people across the country. When one of his young carriers, an African American teen, claimed a white carrier had beaten him, Black readers canceled their subscriptions. But when it was learned the young man had made up the story, the Black readers signed up again as subscribers. Things were not much better, if not worse, at home. A dead dog was thrown on Major's lawn, a bag of shrimp peels and crab shells, and later roofing tacks, were scattered onto his driveway, and his yard rolled with toilet paper. When he received a report from the FBI that his house might be bombed, he stayed up all night on guard with a shotgun. One night as he watched Klansmen plant a wooden cross on his lawn, he raised his borrowed and loaded .38 caliber pistol and rather than fire at another human, aimed several connecting shots into the getaway car. One of his reporters snapped a photo of the fleeing vehicle and later the FBI and police were able to identify the owner, a Klansman.

Yet through all of this, Major and his family never lost their sense of humor. At a gathering at his home one night, the Klan burned another cross on his lawn. His friends jokingly commented that the Majors sure knew how to throw a party. Recollections such as these provide not only a glimpse of life on the front lines but display how a newspaperman with a righteous cause can lead a community through a crisis while protecting his family at home. Major asked of his readers only the things he asked of himself: To obey the laws of the land, to work for the good of all in the community, and to begin the generational work of erasing the evil of racism. Looking back, there is no doubt that Major's resolve and sense of right and wrong were among the reasons the town survived the turmoil. He is an example of how important the role of a journalist and a newspaper are to the progress and life of a community. We also must consider that courageous newspapermen like Lou Major are vanishing as quickly as newspapers. Honest coverage of his community—good and bad—was the theme of Major's career. Who will perform this role in another decade if community newspapers continue to die out?

Major's memoir also touches upon politics, including the leadership of Governor John McKeithen, who was elected to office in 1964 just as the troubles in Bogalusa broke loose. An avowed segregationist when elected, McKeithen evolved on the issue of race mostly because of the troubles he saw in Bogalusa, a place he visited many times during those turbulent years. When a federal official—former Congressman Brooks Hayes—was invited by Major and other moderates in Bogalusa to speak before an integrated audience, McKeithen said the invited guest should stay at home in Arkansas. McKeithen, in part, was trying to protect the city from violence because he knew such a happening could end up in bloodshed, yet his comments undermined the efforts of the newspaper. McKeithen should have supported the meeting and as the days passed it is likely he saw his mistake. The governor's views changed and Major explains the dynamics, both political and social, as the governor worked with city officials to maintain peace and promote law and order. As Major struggled to keep the paper on course with a moderate outlook on race, he realized that he could not cover every racial disturbance that occurred, writing, "My personal responsibility lay more in trying to do whatever I could to keep things cool than publishing every detail of every minor racial incident." But he knew what was most important. When the Civil Rights bill passed in July 1964 on the 50th anniversary of Bogalusa's founding, Major called for respect of the new legislation, noting, "We must live by the laws."

I have spent four years investigating the attack on the two Black deputies outside Bogalusa in 1965. I have looked over thousands of front pages of the *Daily News* from the late 1940s through the late 1960s. Major's coverage of the Civil Rights Era in Bogalusa was exemplary, although some will find problems with his criticisms of CORE. In my view, there was no other editor or publisher in Louisiana, and only a few in the South, who displayed such courage, integrity, and morality in the face of deadly adversity and such life-altering social advances. Major's work should be taught to students studying journalism and community newspapers in Louisiana.

Because he chose not to comment on Bogalusa for decades, Major's decision to recount his work later in life is like uncovering a treasure that has been lost for a half-century, much like recovering FBI documents that shed new light on the era. The memoir is fresh, exciting, moves at a good pace, and is an important account of Louisiana history, civil rights, the South, race relations, journalism, and the value of an outstanding newspaper publisher and editor in a community where one is vitally needed.

—*Stanley Nelson*

ACKNOWLEDGMENTS

In giving my recollections and thoughts on the events in this memoir a place to reside other than my aging mind, it is important that I acknowledge—and deeply thank—the people who were part of those memories from that period and the half-century newspaper career of which those days were a part. The *Bogalusa Daily News,* my "home away from home" for fifty years, was much more than just a building with a press and offices filled with typewriters (and later, computers). It was and continues to be, in its essence, a gathering of wonderful people—at the time of the memories recalled here and for my entire career—who gave their all to their jobs and to the paper. It was easy to think of the *Daily News* as a second home, because the people there have always been "family" who worked together, partied together, celebrated together, and mourned together. During those difficult days in the 1960s, I never felt truly alone when I was with the people who also thought of the *Daily News* as their home away from home. During difficult times, these people did not let threats against the newspaper, and the people associated with it, stop them from soldiering on to make the *Daily News* as good as it could be for the good of the community.

In addition to the local newspaper employees, part of that family was Milton I. Wick, owner of the newspaper and my publishing mentor, who gave me the opportunity to serve the *Daily News,* Bogalusa, and Washington Parish—and later, his sons Walter and Robert Wick who had me join them in leading Wick Communications after their father's death.

The current management of the *Daily News*, now under different corporate ownership than I worked with for fifty years, has been very gracious in allowing the use of editorials, news stories, photos, and letters to the editor from that period. While I may have written the editorials and clipped them and some of the other material from the paper for my stash of memorabilia, that material is, after all, the *Daily News*'s. Without access to the fifty-year-old bound volumes of past editions and use of the material therein, making something sensible from only my memories and a collection of yellowed clippings may not even have been possible.

Also part of the *Daily News* family was Bascom D. Talley Jr., the paper's attorney, landlord, and minority stockholder during that period. More important, he was my advocate when the Wicks needed a new publisher and became my staunch supporter during those trying times. Then and later, he was my dear friend until his passing less than a decade after the events in this memoir.

Most important of all is my wife Peggy, nee Blanche Marguerite Ripp, to whom this collection of memories is dedicated. My high-school sweetheart and the mother of our four wonderful children—Lou Jr., Steven, Christie, and Jason—has been my lifelong partner, companion, confidant, and supporter for more than sixty years. These memories are, in no small part, also hers.

AGAINST
the KLAN

INTRODUCTION

How does a bad story begin?

How does the memory pull up vividly from the past the ugliness it has tried to block out for almost fifty years? Why should it try? Who cares, anyway? Since the ugly Sixties—the 1960s of the twentieth century—the bad story has been told many times in many ways. It has been relived vividly by some, forgotten by others.

For most of those years since then, the stuff I collected from that period has been stuffed away in a box on a closet shelf, or in a drawer here, or a file cabinet there—all in total disarray. For most of those years I did not really care if these recollections ever came to light. Others have done it, many embellished upon it.

But a good friend told me several times through the years that it is important that I write this story—that what happened to me and my newspaper in my town should be told. I imagine I can best label this effort as being "for posterity." If that isn't good reason enough, then I suppose there is no good reason for writing this.

Life in my small town, which could be hate-filled, was in many cases precarious. There were my family and my fortunes—and my company's—to be considered. After all, the story being told here will solve no problems now. What will it accomplish? But as the years have moved on and I have realized that I have used far more of them than I now have left, the big question has always lingered: would I ever sit down and do it at all?

The civil rights struggle in Bogalusa and Washington Parish covered a period of several years that has been extensively written about in published histories and academic papers. This memoir, though, is far more limited in scope: it deals primarily with what I refer to as Bogalusa's "Brooks Hays period" in late 1964 and early 1965, with the follow-on conciliation period by Bogalusa Mayor Jesse Cutrer in the rest of 1965 and 1966 and into 1967, and with the Ku Klux Klan in Bogalusa and Washington Parish during those years.

My memories of this story are supplemented with a large collection of letters to the editor, letters to and from me and others personally, newspaper articles, and my own newspaper editorials. There are the Klan's "Midnight Mails" and other material that seemed pertinent enough at the time that I stuck such into my stash instead of the trash. I wish now that I had saved more.

These various papers give a broader insight into that period of my early career as a newspaper publisher and of the role of the *Daily News* in what was surely the most focused period of racial disorder in the city's history. Other documents of that KKK period lend to further understanding of the issues of the day.

Some of the people who were part of the events of this period are, at the time of this writing, still alive. Some are still in town while others have moved away to other parts. Some of these people have been cordial with me in the years after the hate-filled disagreements of that period, even including some of the former Klansmen and their sympathizers. Time marched on from that period after their cause was lost.

We can never know if, in the intervening years between then and now, those people truly changed their racist attitudes in their own hearts and minds. But at that time, their beliefs were blunted by the force of the federal government and the realization that even local officials would be forced to uphold the law of the land—even if they did not do so willingly.

And the *Daily News* and I could move on to do other things for the people of Bogalusa and Washington Parish, Louisiana.

1

IS THAT A "W" OR AN "N"?

1951–1963

My career as a small town newspaperman began at the Bogalusa, Lou-isiana, *Daily News* following my graduation from the Louisiana State University School of Journalism in Baton Rouge. While the newspaper's incorporated name was the *Bogalusa Daily News*, it was known simply to local residents as the *Daily News* because the name "Bogalusa" did not appear in the banner across the top of page one because the paper's news coverage and distribution area went beyond Bogalusa.

In the "toe" of the Louisiana boot, the *Daily News* served all of Wash-ington Parish: its largest city Bogalusa in the east; the parish seat of Franklinton twenty miles to the west; and the smaller Washington Par-ish communities of Angie, Enon, Mt. Hermon, Pine, Thomas, Varnado, and so many named and unnamed country road intersections in be-tween. The paper also served the communities of Sun and Bush in the northern part of neighboring St. Tammany Parish to the south, and the western edge of Pearl River County, Mississippi, across the Pearl River that is the state line between southeastern Louisiana and neighboring Mississippi only a few miles east of Bogalusa.

Hiring on in July 1951 a few weeks after graduating from the LSU jour-nalism school, I started out writing obituaries, weather reports, and other miscellaneous items before I was thrust into the sports editor's chair due to the illness of then-writer Ned Lyons.

Since I grew up in the racially divided South, in New Orleans and adjacent suburban Jefferson Parish, becoming involved in the coverage of separate all-white and all-black high school sports seemed totally normal for me. I covered the entire high school sports scene in Bogalusa and surrounding Washington Parish with no second thoughts about all of the teams being fully segregated by race.

In the city, there were the all-white Bogalusa High School Lumberjacks and the all-black Central Memorial High School Spartans. Their athletes competed only against other segregated school teams of their own color. I wondered, after several years of writing about these teams, why they didn't play one another, although my thoughts at that time were never put into print.

White football fans attended only Lumberjacks games and Black fans went only to Spartans games. Since both high school football teams played on Friday nights, I was always at the Lumberjacks games. Only once, when the Lumberjacks were not playing on the same night, did I cover one Spartans game in person. But I knew Coach Lucius Jefferson of the Spartans very well because he always accommodated me with full details of their games afterward. The schools' other teams in basketball and baseball were similarly totally segregated.

In the 1950s, life in all its aspects was still similarly divided by color—whether in churches, restaurants, movie houses, or public transportation. It's just the way things were. But in the late 1950s and early 1960s, the Black population of the country began to call for added civil rights. They no longer wanted to have to drink at separate water fountains marked "colored," to be denied service at restaurants, or—in Bogalusa, at least—be forced to enter the movie houses by a separate door that led up the stairs to the balcony where they were allowed to sit.

Black people wanted the right to vote without intimidation and contrived limitations. They wanted to attend the church of their choice and they wanted their children to attend better-funded schools with white children in order to get a better education. They no longer wanted to be forced to sit "at the back of the bus."

But nothing began to change until passage of the Civil Rights Act of 1964. As far as anyone in Bogalusa was concerned, that meant only that schools and restaurants would be integrated. That is a massive generalization, of course, but people who wanted things to stay as they always had been could only interpret the Civil Rights Act in those terms.

It meant that when school opened for the next term, there would be Black children sitting beside white children (full desegregation actually took several years to implement). It meant that Black people could go to the movie house and sit downstairs where the whites did, and they could even use the same front door and drink from the same water fountain. It also meant that Black people would be able to enter and eat in the same restaurants as white people—and at the same time!

And, Lord Almighty, they could even go to a "white man's church" and praise the Lord there, if they wanted to.

The times they were a changin', as Bob Dylan sang that year, and it was a change that would tear through the middle of our small-town, mostly rural-minded society—if, indeed, "society" existed in the piney woods of the Louisiana-Mississippi borderlands.

Long before civil rights was popular as a societal concept and way of life, the *Daily News* played its normal Southern role of recording the news of the day in terms of race. A Black person was a "colored" person in our town, and that's the way the newspaper reported it. A white John Doe was referred to as "Mr. John Doe," receiving that honorific "Mr." even when charged with some heinous crime. A Black John Doe, however, was referred to in the paper with no such honorific. He was "John Doe, colored . . ." It was the way things were done; it was the way most small-town Southern newspapers did it.

After I had been with the newspaper as a "cub" reporter for several years, and following my time at the sports desk, I began covering the police beat. My morning routine after arriving at the office was to head to police headquarters and check the arrest log for the previous day's and night's arrests. One morning, as I was checking the log, there was an entry about the arrest of a man who had been charged with selling lewd and lascivious literature.

Police officers in those days wrote either a "W" or an "N" (White or Negro) in the log next to the name of the person who had been arrested. On that particular morning, I mistook the "W" next to the name of the man arrested for selling bawdy material as an "N" and I went back to the office and wrote the story that way, identifying the arrested man as a "Negro." The paper hit the street that afternoon and I learned my first lesson in carelessness the next morning.

I was sitting at my desk when a man came into the office and was ranting at Hal Houser, my editor and publisher whose no-door office was just behind me. The man was yelling loudly to Houser that he was "not a damned nigger," and he wanted something done about my error that had identified him as one. Houser tried to calm him down, with little success. I wanted to hide, but I dared not get out of my chair.

The man yelled that he was going to sue the *Daily News* for libeling him by calling him a Negro in the police reports. Houser talked with him about the situation for a few minutes and then the offended "literature" salesman left the office. Houser, a very stern publisher and stickler for accuracy, told me he hoped that this would be a lesson for me in the future. Thank goodness he didn't fire me on the spot.

Then Houser contacted the newspaper's attorney and asked for advice. When all was said and done, a settlement was reached. I learned later that the newspaper had given the man $75 and bought him a new suit. The best news was that Houser didn't make me pay for it.

A few years later when I had become publisher, I inherited a newspaper situation that was rather unusual, I suppose—but not so unusual when you consider the time and place.

Each Friday afternoon, we printed what was called the "colored edition" of the *Daily News*—and that had nothing to do with the color of the ink on the newsprint. It was a separate edition of the paper that included a single page dedicated to news stories and photos concerning the town's Black community. After a short start-up pressrun of several hundred issues containing that special page, the press was stopped and the page that was specific to the Black community was removed from the press and replaced by a page of "regular" news containing news about white people. Then the rest of the 8,500-or-so pressrun was completed. There was nothing on the front page or anywhere else in the colored edition to indicate that it was a different edition, other than that single page with news and photos of Black residents.

Those several hundred copies of the colored edition were circulated only in the then-strictly segregated areas of the city and were intended for the eyes of Blacks only. There were absolute and strict safeguards in place to make very sure whites never saw the colored edition. The system of safeguards wasn't failsafe, however, and occasionally the paper received irate phone calls from white subscribers who had received the colored edition of the paper by mistake.

This segregated news edition continued even into the early 1960s. In late 1962, upon becoming publisher of the newspaper, I put an end to it. The few irate phone calls from whites who happened to get a "colored edition" from time to time was nothing compared with the calls we received when I began running news and photos from the Black community intermingled in the single edition of the *Daily News*. Old habits die hard, and there were many who did not want to see "those niggers" in their *Daily News*. But there was no question of returning to the old way, and the newspaper did not suffer from the change beyond the verbal abuse on the phone.

2

THE MARK OF THE CROSS

1963-1964

I had been at the *Daily News* publisher's desk for a little more than a year at the end of 1963, and so much was happening all over the nation in the closing months and weeks of that year. Under the forceful leadership of the Rev. Martin Luther King Jr., the Black citizenry across the country had become a force for social change, and civil rights legislation was moving along in Washington, DC. The assassination of President John F. Kennedy on November 22, 1963, stunned the nation, and Vice President Lyndon B. Johnson assumed the presidency to carry forth. In the months after the assassination, the South seemed even more stunned that now-President Johnson—a Texan and fellow Southerner!—pushed the civil rights legislation to its conclusion. On June 29, 1964, it became law.

It was during those early days of 1964, between the Kennedy killing and the signing of the Civil Rights Act, that racial unrest really began to intensify in Bogalusa.

At one time, the *Daily News* had published on its editorial page columns by both conservative columnist Ralph de Toledano and the more liberal Drew Pearson. However, in the years leading up to civil rights legislation—and when I was not yet the publisher and therefore not involved in making decisions such as which syndicated columnists the paper would carry—the liberal Pearson was "pulled."

In 1963, shortly after I had become publisher, I announced in the paper that the Drew Pearson column would return to the *Daily News*. Some of our Black readers had requested the return of Pearson to the editorial page several times—and even offered to pay for it—and I felt at the time it was journalistically fair to have an opinionated columnist such as Pearson to help balance an editorial page that also featured the archconservative de Toledano. In normal times, this might not have seemed to be a consequential decision, but in the early 1960s, it was a move that most of the white readers of the *Daily News* did not like.

Unrest was being seen all over the South as the wheels had been set in motion to desegregate public schools. On September 4, 1963, there were protests in Hammond, Louisiana. Following the lead of the state capital Baton Rouge, Hammond's mayor announced the formation of a biracial committee on September 9. On September 24, demonstrators were arrested by police in Selma, Alabama.

On October 8, Louisiana labor leader Victor Bussie, a politically strong figure in the state in the 1960s, came to Bogalusa to speak to the local Rotary Club's weekly lunch meeting at the downtown Acme Cafe. Bussie's scheduled speaking engagement was known by the public, and even in this—at the time—strong labor town, he was jeered and told to go home by standers-by on the sidewalk as he entered the cafe to speak to the Rotarians. He was considered too close a follower of President Kennedy and the ideas of racial liberalism. Bussie spoke anyway and left without incident.

About that time, the *Daily News's* editorial "Don't Promote Trouble" was one of the first public acknowledgments that there were racial rumblings in the community, as there were around the nation. It was intended as a simple call for restraint, but its "there's nothing to see here" tone on race relations in the city and parish would soon be proven to be off the mark.

DON'T PROMOTE TROUBLE

For the past several weeks, stories have been floated through Bogalusa about racial demonstrations and integration and trouble here and trouble there. In every instance, it turned out that the "trouble" was nothing more than a rumor or figment of somebody's fertile imagination.

There are those, undoubtedly, who feel that these words do not need to be written. We feel otherwise. We frankly get tired of probing here and there to find out about something which has not happened and something which need not happen if we keep a cool head on our shoulders.

From all we can learn, there is no trouble brewing here. We have very good relations between the races and hope and pray that they may forever continue, in spite of the trouble people are having elsewhere.

Only made-up stories and suppositions by hotheads can change this picture. We must keep our channels of communication open at all times. If there are problems, they can be talked out before there is any serious trouble. But it is reckless foolishness for people to shoot off their mouths about the trouble they have seen when there was no trouble at all . . .

One thing is certain: if you sit by and do nothing while there is trouble all about you, eventually, it will creep your way, arrive and it will be difficult to contain. But by taking positive, yet conservative action, trouble can be kept away. A passive attitude will not get the job done.

But to drum up a concocted tale and try to stir up trouble will certainly result in a bumper crop. We would advise communication, not isolation from the problem.

So, as the New Year rang in January 1964, I still had no idea that my two-year editorial battle with the Ku Klux Klan was looming.

Though I attended St. Aloysius, a Roman Catholic high school in New Orleans, when I was growing up, I attended the local Presbyterian Church near where we lived in suburban Jefferson Parish. So from the time I had moved to Bogalusa in July 1951, my wife Peg and I had attended and been members of the First Presbyterian Church; as a family, we were regular attendees for a dozen years.

What changed that was the testing of local churches' admission policies by Blacks. The practice had become commonplace and First Presbyterian was one of the local churches targeted late in 1963. The church's leadership, however, moved to block the admission of Blacks into the church by adopting a "no blacks" policy. It was sufficient reason for me to stop attending the church. While I hardly deserved the mantle of "flaming liberal," I could not condone denying admission to anyone into a house of worship.

At the time, the Rev. Bruce Shepherd, rector of St. Matthew's Episcopal Church across town in Bogalusa, was a man of high profile in the city. He had been very active in Community Concerts, the civic music association that helped bring in touring classical talent for concerts in the city of more than 20,000 people. I was also involved in Community Concerts, had been a friend of his for some time, and found it easy to move from First Presbyterian to St. Matthew's, thus the entire family moved its membership to Rev. Shepherd's flock.

Rev. Shepherd had to fight the same battles with members in his church as every other preacher or priest in the South had to. On a particular Sunday in January 1964, he asked if I would be an usher because it had been well known in town that Black citizens were going to go to St. Matthew's to try to attend the morning service that Sunday. Some of the regular ushers at the church had let it be known they were not going to allow Blacks to enter.

That's why Rev. Shepherd turned to me; he knew I would not stop anyone at the front door. So the Black visitors came and, as parishioners in the pews stared, made their way to sit near the front for the full service. I had greeted them cordially at the door at the rear of the sanctuary, and there were no incidents of any kind. It had all gone the way that Rev. Shepherd and I and a few others at the church had hoped it would—without incident—and the Black worshippers did not return in later weeks.

At the same time in Washington, DC, the US House of Representatives was passing, by a vote of 290–130, the Civil Rights bill after nine days of debate and action on 138 amendments. It was hailed by President Johnson as a "historic step forward for the cause of human dignity in America." The vote had nothing to do with party lines. Voting for the bill were 152 Democrats and 132 Republicans. Voting against it were 96

Democrats and 34 Republicans. The bill was finally passed after Senate action in July.

The day before the House voted, racial hatred mixed with local politics was spread in Bogalusa. On Thursday, January 9, 1964, someone actually used the *Daily News* to do it, by asking naïve young newspaper delivery boys to deliver a hate sheet along with copies of the paper. So I wrote the following editorial and placed it on page one of the next day's paper on Friday the 10th.

AN UGLY SMEAR

Taking advantage of a child's immaturity, persons unknown yesterday afternoon got at least one *Daily News* paperboy to insert into the *Daily News* a small sheet of racial hate propaganda.

A woman in an automobile called to the paperboy on Washington Street and asked him to deliver one of the sheets of racial filth with each of his papers. The boy was halfway through his route and said he didn't know there was anything wrong with it and took them "to help the lady."

A number of subscribers in the Terrace received the sheet with their *Daily News* yesterday afternoon. Another paperboy turned the woman down in the Brookside Subdivision.

The *Daily News* had no knowledge of this until it was informed by a reader that the sheet was found inside the paper.

This type of practice and the racial hate piece printed are even below the depths of "dirty politics," this obviously being a last-ditch political smear. The *Daily News* abhors this type of practice and everything it stands for. All paperboys were today instructed to deliver nothing with the *Daily News* in the future.

We would appreciate a report of any infractions.

The politics involved in this episode was a hotly contested local election that week for sheriff of Washington Parish, with three-term incumbent Dorman A. Crowe being challenged for the fourth time by the same unsuccessful challenger in the previous three races, former Bogalusa Fire Chief Elmer Smith.

This was the only attempt, to my knowledge, to get our newspaper carriers—many of them young boys on bicycles—to deliver anything of this type with the newspaper. This was not the typical issue of the Midnight Mail, though, because those were usually rolled up tightly and bound with a small rubber band, and it had not been delivered under the cover of darkness.

I had determined at that time, and remained consistent throughout the troublesome years of racial hatred, that the *Daily News* would not publish the substance of what became known as "The Midnight Mail"—a single sheet of racial hatred tossed out of cruising vehicles by the Ku Klux Klan, usually late on Saturday night. Sidewalks and driveways throughout the city bore evidence on countless Sunday mornings that the KKK had been busy distributing their stuff the previous night.

That unauthorized insert into the paper may not actually have been issued by the Klan but by people interested in the sheriff's race who were merely trying to copy the KKK's favorite method of communications. Nevertheless, that episode prompted, at least in part, the editorial that I wrote for the Sunday morning paper following the Saturday election. But I had to write it on Saturday without knowing how that day's vote would turn out. Titled, "A Saturday Editorial on Sunday," it called for civil political discourse instead of hate-filled hostility toward candidates who did not promote certain viewpoints.

As on that day, Louisiana's Saturday elections always caused a problem for our Sunday edition—which, unlike our weekday afternoon editions, was a morning edition. Readers wanted their paper waiting for them on the front steps or in the driveway when they got up on Sunday morning. To manage this, the press usually rolled at midnight on Saturday in order to be ready for distribution in the predawn darkness. We were even able to get in the Saturday night football results with a midnight press time.

But election Saturdays were different. Most states vote on Tuesdays, but in Louisiana all state and local elections are on Saturday. The polls didn't close until 8:00 p.m., and our reporters had to wait at the Parish Courthouse in Franklinton for the final tally—often delayed when results from this precinct or that were delayed—and then start digesting and writing the results for the front-page headlines and stories. The press never rolled at midnight on election Saturday nights; instead of the paper waiting for the readers in the dark as on most Sunday mornings, many readers were up and waiting for the paper to be delivered to them in the early morning sunshine.

By the time the paper hit the streets on this Sunday morning—with the election results on page one—Crowe had beaten Smith yet again to win his fourth and final term. That term would include his hiring of Oneal Moore and Creed Rogers as Washington Parish's first Black sheriff's deputies. Then, as the parish's top law enforcement officer, he would preside a year later over the aftermath of a nighttime ambush that left Deputy Moore dead and Deputy Rogers wounded.

At the same time, area Ku Klux Klan activity had begun to intensify. On January 18, 1964, there was a widespread planting of burning crosses in the Florida Parishes, the collection of parishes that stretched from the state capital in Baton Rouge on the west to Washington Parish and the Pearl River on the east. Before Louisiana became a state in 1812, this area had briefly been a part of the West Florida Republic and is still referred to regionally as the Florida Parishes.

The outbreak of fiery crosses from Bogalusa to near Baton Rouge came at about 11:00 p.m. on that Saturday night. All of the crosses were constructed the same way, made from lengths of 2 × 4 lumber and wrapped in gasoline-soaked burlap. Most also had a metal spike in the bottom of the cross's upright section, which made it easier for Klansmen to quickly thrust it into the ground, light it, and escape into the darkness.

Bogalusa Police on Saturday night credited the cross plantings to youths, but by Monday morning they had changed their tune and admitted that adults must have been responsible given the quality of the construction and the extent of the lightings across several hundred square miles of the state.

A total of eight crosses were burned within the Bogalusa city limits that night. Others were burned in areas north of the city in northeast Washington Parish around the villages of Varnado and Angie, where there was a concentrated Black population. In all, more than 150 burning crosses were set out that night in southeastern Louisiana, an impressive display by the Original Knights of the Ku Klux Klan.

It was the first time a Klan cross was burned in front of my home at 240 Camellia Road. There would be more.

The Klan issued a Midnight Mail "explaining" the symbolism—to them—of burning crosses: "The burning symbolizes destroying the cross instead of Christ. The Jews who were responsible for the crucifixion of Christ have enslaved the people of Europe and Asia, are on the march in this country determined to destroy the White race and Western culture. Many of our so-called Christian churches are following Jewish Talmudic teachings instead of the New Testament. Our schools are being subverted by One World Jewish philosophies."

It went on to declare, "The Klan will disband and return to normal life only when the American government is back under White Christian control . . . ," and closed with, in all caps: "IF AMERICA MUST BE SAVED FROM UNDERGROUND THE KLAN GOES UNDERGROUND."

United Press International, reporting on the incidents, noted that "cross burnings and Klan statements have become increasingly evident across Louisiana during the past year, but slacked off during the recent gubernatorial election in which John McKeithen, an avowed segregationist, defeated deLesseps S. Morrison, who is generally considered a moderate on the racial question." McKeithen had served on the state Public Service Commission from a district in north central Louisiana; Morrison was a former mayor of New Orleans.

Initially, in the 1960s, I wondered why I had been labeled in the Midnight Mails by those with racial hatred in their hearts as such a flaming liberal—even as a "Communist." The elimination of the "colored edition" of the paper and the resumption of Drew Pearson's column might have been just enough reason for the Klan. And there definitely was my association with Bogalusa attorney Bascom Destrehan Talley Jr., as Southern-bred and Southern-born as they come, but definitely thought of as being in the liberal camp by 1963–64 Southern standards.

Talley was the most successful attorney in Bogalusa and the head man of one of the largest law firms in Washington Parish. His firm was known to be friendly to Black people and their needs and thus counted many Blacks among its clientele. Talley was well known and respected with the bar of Louisiana and he had a huge number of political and legal contacts throughout the state and nation. His contacts reached into the heart of Washington, DC, and among his closest allies was US Congressman James H. "Jimmie" Morrison of Hammond. He was on a first-name basis with many politicos of the state and nation, including the powerful US Senator Russell B. Long from north Louisiana.

Many Bogalusa people were jealous of Talley's success, his money, and his power and influence. Independently well-off and later among the founders of a national bank in Bogalusa, he was one of those people who seemed to be invulnerable. The fact that he befriended Blacks made him a perfect target for the Klan.

My association with him resulted from the fact that he was not only the *Daily News*'s attorney—the one who settled the paper's matter that resulted in $75 and a suit for the white man I mistakenly identified as Black—but he was also a minority stockholder in the newspaper. In earlier years, Talley had mortgaged his house to pump money into a failing *Daily News*, which was founded in 1927. His money and support helped keep the paper afloat until the time that Publisher Halford Houser came on the scene from Indiana. A solid newspaperman with the highest of journalistic ethics, Houser led the newspaper to complete respectability.

Because Talley was also landlord of the building that housed the paper's offices and press, many in the community had the mistaken impression that the *Daily News* belonged to him. While he actually owned only 15 percent of the stock, his high profile and frequent stop-in visits to the newspaper led many in the community to believe his ownership and influence were much greater than they were.

For some, the notion that Talley was the boss at the *Daily News* lived long after the 1960s. In his 2004 book the *Deacons for Defense: Armed Resistance and the Civil Rights Movement,* author Lance Edward Hill wrote that Talley was publisher of the *Daily News* and that I was the editor. While I was the editor when Houser was publisher, when I became publisher after Houser I was dual-hatted as Editor and Publisher—handling the business side of the paper as publisher as well as overseeing the paper's news coverage as editor. The majority of the stock in the newspaper was owned by two brothers named Milton and Jim Wick who lived in Arizona and Washington, DC. Talley held his 15 percent of the stock and owned the building that housed the newspaper, and he was the paper's lawyer. But he was never the publisher.

I must acknowledge that it was Talley, who became a dear friend, who helped me rise to the publisher's chair at the *Daily News* and get through those tough early years of me being a publisher. That's the reason I didn't mind being linked with him in those scurrilous Midnight Mails that the Klan threw in the city's driveways on so many Saturday nights—that and not caring what the Klan thought of me in the first place.

Talley and Houser were cordial, but I don't think they were very close. Upon my graduation from LSU, Houser hired me to come to work as a $45-a-week "cub" reporter at the *Daily News,* and I worked for him for more than ten years. I would see Talley from time to time when he came by the office.

Two publishers followed Houser with short stints at the *Daily News:* Don R. Hancock and Harold Wilson. I succeeded Wilson in June 1963, probably primarily because of Bascom Talley. As the paper's minority stock holder, he touted me to the paper's two primary owners, the out-of-state Wick brothers. It was Talley who urged the Wicks to give me a chance once they made the decision to end Wilson's tenure as publisher.

Whereas Houser had been my mentor upon joining the *Daily News,* Bascom Talley was my patron with the Wicks. We genuinely liked each other, and there was a close bond. He helped me and encouraged me at every turn. At the young age of thirty-three, I became publisher of a daily newspaper—and at a very tumultuous time in the Deep South.

The Talleys also got a cross on that January night in 1964. The crosses burned early on Saturday night, and the public had a chance to read about them in the Sunday paper the next morning because we had a late pressrun time on Saturday nights to get Saturday night's sports results into the Sunday edition. Following the news story on Sunday, on Monday I wrote an editorial about the burning crosses and their cowardly perpetrators that ran in the Tuesday edition:

THE MARK OF THE CROSS

The old sign of the Ku Klux Klan, the flaming cross, charred the land of southeastern Louisiana this past weekend and it is hard not to recall the day when Jesus Christ was shamed in death on another cross hundreds of years ago.

Isn't it a pitiful thing that there are still people living among us in our daily lives who still have to resort to sneaking around under the cover of night to spread their hate and terror? We refrain calling these people "men" because they do not deserve such determination . . .

We wonder whether these night-riders think of the feelings of children and wives in homes where they planted their dirty flaming crosses. Obviously, they are people without conscience, bent only on spreading fear.

The name of the group which did the work is only incidental to the act itself. Their crosses carried out partially what they were intended to. They got attention, as naturally they would. They caused a stir and left the people wondering who would do such a thing and why.

. . . [P]eople of sound mind and principles can find little more in the cross burnings than a message of unprincipled hate for mankind. Unfortunately, the people responsible are living and working in our midst every day, are people of obvious low mentality without any scruples.

They need to be exposed to the light of day and shamed for their heinous actions. But more than despised, these people need to be pitied. They have not kept with civilization. They are throwbacks to a day when rash emotionalism ruled over reason. We pray the night-riders may grow up into men of God-fearing conscience before they are called on to answer for their terror tactics which leave a mark on children, wives and decent, law-abiding humanity.

Looking back, that must have been my "shot heard round the Klan's world." I wrote what I felt about hatred and the way the Ku Klux Klan tried to intimidate law-abiding citizens who were only trying to do in their lives what was right and just. But if the Ku Klux Klan and their supporters had needed to reach deep to find a valid reason to have a personal hatred for me before January 21, 1964, that editorial probably settled the matter for them.

The following two weeks brought a number of responses, by way of letters to the editor, to that editorial.

A Bogalusa woman wrote:

Your editorial "Mark of the Cross" in Tuesday's *Daily News* left me nauseous. . . . I feel these crosses to us are a reminder that we should be striving harder to preserve freedom. . . . Who are you to say this was hate and not dissention [*sic*]. . . . Evidently someone feels you are a leftist, otherwise you would feel no fear or resentment from burning crosses.

Another reader asked:

. . . Isn't it a shame that in our daily lives we read a newspaper that prints what it wants its readers to read and not necessarily what the reader would prefer to read. News media has a very unique way of leading people to think in their terms. How does John Q. Citizen reflect his views to other people? Has it ever occurred to you that the burning of crosses may be his only way? Have you ever published an editorial which would lead people to believe something contrary to your own beliefs?

Still another wrote:

We, the white race, have been taught segregation from our youth up and [it] is hard for us to depart from. The Ku Klux Klan may be the one means we have to resort to help us retain our way of life and the way we have been taught from our youth up.

And a tongue-in-cheek letter writer using a fictitious name asked for the *Daily News*'s help in joining the Klan so he could "feel the arsonistic thrill and excitement from flicking my Zippo under the arms of a kerosene-saturated cross planted on some unbeliever's lawn."

At the time we did not know that the writer was not a real person, and soon after, when we had found out, we ran under the "Letters to the Editor" heading the following item that every newspaper editor hates to have to write:

The *Daily News* wishes to state publicly that, to its knowledge, there is no such person in or around Bogalusa as Joal Johnson, over whose name two letters to the editor have appeared recently. There is also no Post Office Box number as 311, which the writer submitted as his (or her) address at the Bogalusa Post Office. The *Daily News* asks that fictitious names not be used on Letters to the Editor and it is not, nor has it been, the policy of this paper to run letters with fictitious names. We ask that all readers comply with this policy and do not submit unsigned letters or letters using fictitious names and addresses.

And, a little too late, we started checking letter writers' names and addresses more carefully.

In contrast to the nasty letters I received, about a month later came some praise from one reader:

The only qualification I have to appraise a newspaper or editor is the fact that I am an avid newspaper reader. It is my honest opinion that this community has a good daily newspaper. . . . In my judgment the

Daily News wears blinders in presenting the news. It features both conservative and liberal columnists. The editorial column is informative, moderate, very seldom controversial unless it appears to be in the public interest to be. . . . It has an open policy in printing letters to the editor. Anyone who has read the "letters" column knows this. The *Daily News* publishes the "brickbats" as well as the "bouquets." . . . The editor of the *Daily News* says he loves Louisiana and Bogalusa and has no intention of being run out by mob force. It isn't too difficult to separate the men from the boys after all.

3

A COURSE OF RACIAL MODERATION

1964

While the local cross burnings were obviously page-one headline news, I had set the newspaper on a course of racial moderation months before. Most news of racial protest and confrontations was published on the inside pages of the *Daily News*. Not every schoolyard skirmish between a white and Black child found their way into the newspaper, even though there was constant agitation for us to print every detail of every single racial flare-up, no matter how minor it might have been.

I was determined I would not do this, even at the risk of being accused of censoring the news.

Bogalusa's Black population complained at the time that their marches and pickets and boycotts were being given short shrift in the paper. In the 2003 movie *Deacons for Defense*, about the group of Bogalusa Blacks who took up arms in self-defense against the Klan, a member of the group complains: "The newspapers don't even take pictures of us, so how are we going to get national exposure?"

While exposure in the national media may have been foremost in the Deacons' minds, they were probably also thinking of the *Daily News*. While there were numerous civil rights marches through the city in that period, only one photo of marchers ever made it onto page one of the *Daily News,* and coverage of the civil right movement—locally or nationally—was not always day-to-day or on the front page.

I felt there was an overriding factor in the life and times of the people of Bogalusa and Washington Parish: my personal responsibility lay more in trying to do whatever I could to keep things cool than in publishing every detail of every racial incident.

The Midnight Mail that the Klan distributed fell into the same category. We never—not once—acknowledged the presence of the Midnight Mail in the 1960s, although it was the Klan's primary means of getting out its message of racial hatred. But they certainly acknowledged the *Daily News*, and me, in many of their "editions."

As Klan activities were heating up close to home, on March 9 the US Senate began debating the Civil Rights bill that had been passed by the House of Representatives a month before. The same day, a Black student, John Frazier, was barred from registering for college at the University of Southern Mississippi, about sixty miles away in Hattiesburg.

Louisiana Governor-elect McKeithen was reported as saying the next day that he would stand in the school doorway to block further integration in Louisiana. His vow presaged the now-notorious stance that Alabama Governor George Wallace took three months later, when he defiantly and famously stood in the doorway of a classroom building at the University of Alabama to block Black students James A. Hood and Vivian Malone from attending class. But in the face of 100 National Guard troops who had been called up by President Lyndon Johnson to back up the federal officials who were assisting Hood and Malone, Wallace eventually stepped aside and let the students pass. And, despite his vow, Governor McKeithen never stood in a school doorway to block integration the way Governor Wallace did.

During most of the spring of 1964, there was a very unsettled feeling in and around Bogalusa. Area residents were obviously looking to the future and hoping it wouldn't bring to Bogalusa the violence that was occurring elsewhere. But those area residents were also looking over their shoulders back in time, with the knowledge that the city, parish, and adjacent areas already had a long history of racially motivated violence.

In 1884, sixteen-year-old Huie Conerly, who was Black, was taken from the Washington Parish Jail in Franklinton and lynched on the jailhouse steps after he was accused of attempted rape of an elderly white woman. A "Vigilance and Regulating Committee" left his body hanging there, with a note claiming responsibility. In neighboring St. Tammany Parish, the newspaper there reported that the lynching was "what might have been expected, all things considered. According to information we have received, there were no extenuating circumstances to entitle him to protection or mercy. . . . The universal sentiment is that Conerly has received his just desserts."

On October 27, 1901, a "race riot" left ten dead in the Balltown community in northeastern Washington Parish, where hundreds of Blacks from up and down the lower Pearl River valley were participating in a weeklong church "camp meeting" at Duncan's Chapel. Tensions were high because a day before the start of the camp meeting, on Wednesday, October 23, a local Black man, Bill Morris, had been burned at the stake for an alleged assault on a local white woman.

On that autumn Sunday afternoon, when a local constable and a posse rode into the camp to inquire about a permit that was required for the gathering, the camp meeting crowd was on edge after the Wednesday burning of Morris at the stake, and a member of the posse was shot in the head from the crowd. The resulting shoot-out left ten Blacks dead. When word of the event spread, hundreds of armed white men went to the scene from all over Washington Parish and neighboring Mississippi, but Washington Parish Sheriff Norman H. Simmons and Clerk of Court J. K. Johnson arrived and calmed the crowd before any further slaughter occurred.

In a Pennsylvania newspaper report on the event, the bottom subhead of a four-deck headline read: "For Twenty-Four Hours It Looked as if a Negro Would Not Be Left Alive in Washington Parish."

On Saturday, November 22, 1919, labor troubles in Bogalusa led to the killing of four workers—two white and two Black—of the Great Southern Lumber Company sawmill that was the precursor of today's paper mill in the heart of the city. The "Bogalusa Massacre of 1919" occurred when white sawmill company supporters organized the Self-Preservation and Loyalty League to "self-preserve" white advantage in the mill through "loyalty" to the company. These "enforcers" went to the local Black union office where the International Union of Timber

Workers was organizing Black sawmill workers. The resulting shootout resulted in the deaths of the four union organizers.

The next day, Sunday, November 23, 1919, a rape incident in Bogalusa led to the lynching of an innocent Black man. Placide Butler was fresh off his shift at the Great Southern Lumber Company's sawmill in the heart of the city. He couldn't have been at the rape scene based on the timing of his work shift, but tracking dogs led a posse to the boardinghouse where Butler had just returned from work. As the only person at the Black boarding house at the time, Butler was grabbed by a white mob, dragged through the city streets by a rope around his neck, and hung over a bonfire that burned in the middle of the city's main business street.

In Franklinton in 1935, a gang of white men lynched Jerome Wilson, a young Black man who had been involved in a violent dispute at the Wilson family farm north of town on July 21, 1934. A livestock inspector went there on a matter of dipping the farm's mules as part of a state tick-eradicating effort. A deputy sheriff was killed in a shoot-out, and a week later Wilson was tried and convicted. He was still being held in the Washington Parish Jail in Franklinton a few months later when an appeal overturned his conviction, and local white men took matters into their own hands. They went to the jail and killed Wilson, then took his body and dumped it in a ditch north of the parish seat.

On April 24, 1959, a similar event began in Poplarville, Mississippi, twenty-five miles east of Bogalusa, and ended at the Pearl River—the state line between Louisiana and Mississippi at Bogalusa's eastern edge. A twenty-three-year-old Black man, Mack Charles Parker, was in jail in Poplarville, accused of raping a pregnant white woman. On that Friday night, while he was in jail awaiting his trial that was scheduled to start on the following Monday morning, a posse of about ten masked men got into the jail. They beat and kidnapped Parker, drove him west to the bridge that spans the Pearl River, shot him twice in the chest at close range, weighted his body with logging chains, and dumped him into the Pearl River below. His body was found ten days later, more than two miles downstream from the bridge.

A county grand jury in Poplarville and then a federal grand jury in Biloxi both refused to indict anyone in the lynching despite evidence collected by the FBI. A Poplarville resident said at the time, "You couldn't convict the guilty parties if you had sound film of the lynching." The case remains unprosecuted to this day.

From that event—which one historian called "the last classic lynching in America"—it was only a leap forward of a few years to Bogalusa's period of racial unrest in the early and middle 1960s.

. . . .

On Sunday, April 12, 1963, the Klan temporarily moved away from racial terror and beat a white man who they accused of not supporting his children. The man, estranged from his wife, was grabbed by three hooded men that night on his way to work at the local paper mill, then owned by the Crown Zellerbach corporation.

They struck him on the head with a pistol before shoving him into the backseat of a waiting car and drove him to a remote section of the "company pasture," a vast pine forest that is continuously planted, harvested, and replanted to provide the pulpwood that the mill feeds into its paper-making machines. In those woods, the man said, his abductors flung him over the hood of the car and belt-whipped him.

The victim said he had been providing support for his children, but his protests to the Klansmen fell on deaf ears. The assailants then drove him back to his house near Bogalusa and shoved him out into his yard. Police never found the assailants.

A week later a personal warning came to me. The Ku Klux Klan sent word by way of a beaten television reporter that I had better leave the state of Louisiana or I would suffer the same fate as the reporter. The Monday, April 20, edition of the *Daily News* carried the story under a page-one banner headline, "Klansmen Threaten *Daily News* Publisher." The headline was not for my own self-glorification; it was to keep the public mindful of the KKK's terror tactics.

"*Daily News* Editor and Publisher Lou Major received a warning last night from the Ku Klux Klan that he would be beaten if he did not leave the state," the story began.

It continued with a recounting of a visit by Bob Wagner, a Baton Rouge correspondent for a New Orleans television station, to a Klan gathering the previous Sunday afternoon near Jackson, Louisiana. He was spotted by some Klansmen who were guarding the rural meeting site, set upon, and beaten.

And he was given a message to bring back to me. After the beating, the Klansmen told him to pass along a warning to me that I would "get the same" if I did not leave Louisiana.

But not all of the messages to me were threatening. A few weeks after the critical letters to the editor that followed the cross burnings, a Varnado woman wrote me a letter, which she asked not to be published, urging caution on my part: "Please, please be careful, Mr. Major. As long as you can, please don't print anything about the Klan. Don't publish any letters for or against them. It is a hard fact that they ARE here, ARE organized, and some fool MIGHT take it in his head to 'get even' with you."

The move to university integration in Louisiana continued on June 10 with the enrollment of fifteen Blacks for the summer session at Louisiana State University in Baton Rouge. Two Blacks also registered at Northeast Louisiana University in Monroe. Despite his earlier vow, McKeithen was not there to stand in the doorway to block them, as Wallace did in Alabama the very next day.

As the US Senate passed the Civil Rights bill on Friday, June 19, and sent it back to the House, racial terrorism continued unabated. Five days after the Senate passed the bill, President Johnson ordered 200 US Marines to upstate Mississippi on June 24 to begin searching in Neshoba County for three missing civil rights activists: white students Andrew Goodman, twenty, and Mickey Schwerner, twenty-four, of New York, and twenty-one-year-old James Chaney, a Black student from Meridian, Mississippi.

They were in the area working with a program to register Blacks to vote and had been arrested near Philadelphia, Mississippi, on a speeding charge, jailed, and let go. But they had been missing from the time they were let out of jail, and the station wagon in which they were traveling was found burned shortly after they went missing.

The next day, a racial street battle broke out in St. Augustine, Florida, continuing the no-pattern outbreak of violence around the country.

On May 30, the KKK staged a rally in Bogalusa attended by about 800 Klansmen. Many of the crowd wore Klan robes and hoods. Wearing hoods to conceal one's identity violated city and state antimasking laws, but police made no arrests.

On Thursday, July 2, 1964, after the US House and Senate had agreed to the final details of the Civil Rights Act and sent it on to the White House, President Johnson signed the Civil Rights Act of 1964 into law.

Following the Independence Day holiday on Saturday, the *Daily News* observed the signing in a July 7 editorial about living by the rule of law.

THE ORDERLY PROCESS OF LAW

The major issue of the 20th Century has been the civil rights movement in the United States of America. The people of this nation face a period when sound, reflective logic must prevail.

The United States Congress has passed the controversial Civil Rights Bill. It has been signed into law by the President of the United States. It has become the law of the land.

There has been, at the same time, an outcry for obeying the law and ignoring it. There are many and varied reasons from both sides of the argument. But the main principle which must be observed in this country is that we are a government of law and not of men. Traditions are not easy to give up. Ways of life are not easily set aside. Change is always difficult to accept, regardless of the question involved.

But we must all realize the importance and necessity of obeying the laws—not just the laws which we like or suit us—but all the laws. A person who does not agree with the purpose of stop signs cannot willfully go out and drive through stop signs. Well, in a nation of free men, we cannot deliberately disobey the law and hope to remain free.

There are objectionable points to the Civil Rights law, both to people of the South and people from other areas of the nation. Protests must be handled in an orderly law-abiding manner. Men cannot take the law into their own hands. Where this is done, there is chaos and strife . . .

We must live by laws. We must exercise reason. We cannot allow ourselves to drag fist-fighting and bottle-throwing into our streets. There are processes of law which must be followed in a free, democratic society such as our own . . . Our appeal is that our people remain law-abiding citizens, not only for the laws we like, but for all our laws. If, by orderly process of law, changes are made in national legislation, so be it. But we can ill afford to do battle in the streets.

Let us live by our laws. They are the only hope for a democratic society.

Bogalusa was incorporated on July 4, 1914, so in 1964, two days after the President had signed the historic bill into law, the city celebrated its fiftieth anniversary as a city on the Fourth of July, a Saturday. For a short period of time the celebration helped take the minds of many local residents off of the underlying racial strife in the city. But on the day of our editorial three days later, the holiday and anniversary celebration seemed years away.

On that Tuesday afternoon, two Black girls entered the local F. W. Woolworth variety store (commonly referred to as "Woolworth's") on Columbia Street in the downtown area and sat down at the store's lunch counter, where they were served. Two white girls and a white man were also seated at the counter and there were no incidents and no words spoken to one another.

After word of that event spread, on the next afternoon, July 8, a group of fifteen to twenty white men gathered in front of Woolworth's. The Daily News was told that several of the men had gone to the store earlier in the day and asked the manager about the store policy on seating and serving Blacks (the men actually used the N-word in their inquiry).

The manager told them he would follow the law, and there was no law against serving Black people at the store. One of the men told the manager that if he had known that the Blacks were going to go in to be served the day before, it would not have been allowed to take place.

That same night, white men congregated in front of the Acme Cafe, next to Woolworth's, and there was a simultaneous gathering of other white men in a public parking lot on First Avenue—later to be renamed as Dr. Martin Luther King Jr. Drive—behind the Rosenblum's clothing store, which was across Columbia Street from Woolworth's. Rosenblum's had a back entrance from the parking lot on First Avenue, and the store was used by many as a pass-through from the parking lot to other stores on Columbia Street. Rosenblum's did not object to people using the store as a shortcut; they likely thought it was good for business for people to see their merchandise on the way to and from their cars in the back parking lot.

The next day was to be a veritable powder keg in the city—but one which did not explode.

At 9:15 in the morning, a group of Black people entered the Walgreen's Drug Store, also across the street from the Woolworth's store. Walgreen's had served Black people at its own lunch counter the day before, but when the Blacks went in to sit down at the lunch counter a second day, the owner immediately closed the store and served no one. The Blacks went across the street to the Woolworth's lunch counter, were served, and left.

Shortly afterward, a gang of about fifteen white teenaged boys showed up on Columbia Street waving Confederate flags. They went into the Woolworth's store and were served at the lunch counter while they continued to display their flags. After the boys left the store, two Black girls went inside and were also served. They didn't stay long, however, when they saw the white teens returning. I was told later that the girls had been in town from Slidell for a funeral. Down the block, the Rexall pharmacy, which also had a lunch counter, did not open for business that day.

Later in the morning, about fifty to sixty white men congregated on Columbia Street and milled around, many possibly from the paper mill behind Columbia Street because it was the noon lunch hour. By 12:20 p.m., between twelve and fifteen white men were still outside the Acme Cafe. There was a report that someone in the crowd told a white man who was about to enter the neighboring Woolworth's store, "You'd better not go in there," and the man heeded the warning and left without entering.

A block away, two Black boys who were further down Columbia Street said they were told by a man that there was a place for them in this town—on East Fourth Street (at the edge of a nearby Black residential area)—and that's where they'd better go. The man reportedly told them that if they were looking for trouble, they would find it right there on Columbia Street. The two youths left quickly.

That afternoon, I received a phone call at the office telling me that there were going to be pickets in front of the Woolworth's store at about four o'clock. Fifteen minutes later, a group of seven men came into the *Daily News* office and asked to see me. The leader was one of several people who had been charged with disturbing the peace and trespassing in the nearby community of Varnado several weeks earlier in connection with charges filed against another man for allegedly contributing to the delinquency of a minor.

The group's leader came into my open-doored office and asked if the planned picketing was going to be in the *Daily News* the next day. I told him if anything happened, a story would be in the paper. He then asked me if any photos would be taken and I told him, "No." The man then asked me about the charges filed in Varnado and I told him how we got the information: from the Washington Parish Sheriff's Department. He asked if I would sign an affidavit to that effect and I told him I wasn't going to sign anything, that my word was good. He said, "That's okay" and then left.

At 4:30 that afternoon, downtown Bogalusa was crowded with people. There had been a traffic jam downtown almost all day long as the curious kept driving down Columbia Street and circling the block to do it again, to see what would happen next. Confederate flags were everywhere in sight, carried by men and boys in the street and being waved from the windows of passing cars and pickup trucks.

I brought a pistol—a nine-shot .22 caliber revolver—back to work from home with me at lunchtime and planned to carry it with me to and from home from then on.

That same night, at 8:25 p.m., Bogalusa Mayor Jesse H. Cutrer Jr. telephoned me at my house and asked me if I could come to City Hall. I immediately drove to his office and it was only the two of us.

While Cutrer had made his place in Bogalusa as the owner-operator of the Red Bird Ice Cream Company, as a young man he had made a name for himself in the same field I was in—journalism. A native of Kentwood in neighboring Tangipahoa Parish, in 1934 he was a student in the LSU School of Journalism and was editor of the J-school's student newspaper, the *Daily Reveille.*

While Cutrer was editor, the *Reveille* planned to publish an article critical of Huey Long, the powerful former governor of Louisiana who, at the time, was a US senator preparing to campaign for president. Long got wind of the planned article, contacted the LSU administration and had the article spiked. Cutrer and six other journalism students who were on the paper's staff resigned in protest and left a sign—"Killed by Suppression"—on the door of the *Reveille* office as they left. For their protest, Cutrer and the others were expelled from LSU, but they were subsequently admitted to the prestigious journalism school at the University of Missouri.

After he graduated, Cutrer didn't go into the newspaper business, but came to Bogalusa, became a successful businessman with a local dairy, and was elected mayor in 1962 just as very troubled times in the city were beginning. After one term in office during very challenging times he declined to run for reelection in 1966, and he parlayed his experience in the dairy-ice cream business into a position as executive director of the Louisiana Milk Commission, He died in 1987 at age 72.

The City Hall, now on the National Register of Historic Places, is a stately neoclassical edifice with huge two-story columns at the front portico. After Cutrer's call to me that July 9 evening, I walked through the empty City Hall lobby and down the side hall into the mayor's office and found him on the phone talking with Curt Siegelin, owner of the WIKC radio station in town. Siegelin had been mayor before Cutrer, and he would return to the mayor's office when Cutrer finished his one term.

When he got off the phone, Cutrer asked me if the *Daily News* would cooperate with a strict local news blackout on the racial unrest. I agreed, but on one condition: that the local police would make some effort to clear away the mobs which had gathered in front of Woolworth's, the Acme Cafe, and other Columbia Street stores—those only a block away from the newspaper office—earlier that day. He asked how this could be done, and I told him to just tell the police to do their jobs and move into the crowd and tell everyone to go home. He asked what the mob could be charged with if they didn't disperse, and I suggested disturbing the peace and inciting to riot.

The mayor agreed and said that the police would try to clear away any crowds that might gather on Friday, the next day. He wondered if I thought anybody else might be able to handle the situation better than the police. After thinking for a moment, he answered his own question and said he would go downtown and ask the crowd to move on if they gathered. He also told me he would talk to the Klan group and ask them to try to keep their people away.

Cutrer also told me he had received a registered letter from Ronnie Moore, secretary of the Congress of Racial Equality (CORE) in Louisiana, asking for a meeting with the mayor. He said he would not meet with Moore but would instead ask Andrew Moses, a local Black businessman who was perceived to be moderate on the issue of race relations, to contact Moore and tell him that he, Moses, would meet with Moore, and Moses would then relay the points of discussion to Cutrer.

Cutrer then telephoned Ralph Blumberg, owner of the other radio station in town, WBOX. Blumberg had also agreed to the racial news blackout for four days, the same condition to which Siegelin of WIKC had agreed. With the *Daily News* and both local radio stations in place for the news blackout and Cutrer planning to go downtown to try to disperse any crowds, the mayor seemed to be satisfied at that point that the situation could be cooled down.

On the way home from City Hall that night, however, I heard WIKC repeat that day's news broadcast about the Columbia Street picketing and crowd gathering of earlier in the day. The news report came on at 9:30 p.m. and 10:00 p.m. and was again on WIKC the next morning at 6:00, 6:45, and 8:00 a.m. The news blackout seemed to be over before it had even started.

Friday, July 10, was another day of tension. Crowds of white men began gathering in front of the Acme Cafe early that morning. This time, however, right at 9:00 a.m., a large group of city police arrived downtown and told everybody to clear the streets, as Mayor Cutrer and I had discussed the previous evening. It happened quickly and without incident. Two young boys remained, however, carrying picket signs in front of the Woolworth's store.

Later in the day, the signs were in the hands of two white men. Their signs read "Woolworth Lunch Counter Integrated—Bogalusa Rifle Club." The Woolworth's lunch counter did not open at all that day, but the picketing continued. At 3:00 p.m., the Woolworth's manager got a phone call from somebody who apologized for the picketing, the male caller saying they had only just learned that the counter had not been open all day long. Ten minutes later, an unknown man came and spoke to the picketers, who then left. The Rexall's drugstore and Walgreen's drugstore lunch counters across the street and down the block also remained closed that day.

That night, a crowd of men once again gathered on Columbia Street. There was a minor incident at the Ritz Theater movie house when several young Blacks wanted to sit downstairs, which was historically reserved for white people. Blacks had to use a side door and stairway and sit in the balcony. The theater management refused to admit them downstairs that night.

During the day, Andrew Moses and another local Black moderate, McClurie Sampson, had gone to New Orleans and met with CORE Field

Secretary Moore. Moses advised the CORE official that the local Black people could handle the local situation, and Moore pledged that CORE would not come to Bogalusa.

The most amusing, yet pathetic, occurrence up to that point was a telephone call I received at home that night. An unidentified caller said, "I've lived here all my life and never thought I would see white men picketing in front of a store that just had its lunch counter integrated and they would be bragging about it being integrated." I told the man that the picket signs were not meant to be bragging about the counter being integrated but, rather, were a protest against the integration. "Oh, I see," the caller said before he hung up.

On Saturday morning, July 11, Bogalusa police again showed up downtown. The news blackout had apparently taken hold, as neither of the radio stations was reporting on the local situation. While I was at the office just a half-block off Columbia Street, working on the edition for the following Sunday morning, a man called my house, and when my ten-year-old son Steven answered the phone he was told to tell me that "Two niggers can make news, but not us white people. But tell him we closed down the cafe."

During those few days, we lost six subscribers in the rural Lee's Creek area south of town. They all said that they had been told that a *Daily News* reporter named "Bill" had helped integrate the Woolworth's lunch counter. One of our paper carriers said he had been told the same thing. But we didn't even have a reporter named Bill, and nobody from the *Daily News* had any involvement with the lunch counter integration.

Temporarily, with the mobs off the street, there was a nervous calm through the city.

On July 22, 1964, a group named the "Bi-Racial Committee" made what it called its first annual report to the Bogalusa Citizens Voters League, a group that represented Black interests in the city. The report capsuled what had been happening within the Black community to try to gain more rights for Blacks in the community.

The members of the "Bi-Racial Committee" were all recognized in the city as being among the more moderate of Black leaders. The irony, though, was that this "bi-racial" committee was all-black. Where were the white members?

The committee's report to the Voters League gave interesting details on what was happening around the city from the perspective of its Black residents. It was something of a checklist of problems perceived by the Blacks, solutions requested by the Bi-Racial Committee, and the results. It concluded, "We feel that our accomplishments this first year have been a major breakthrough in race relations. We look forward to bigger and better things."

At the same time, race riots and looting were occurring in Brooklyn, New York, and across the Hudson River in Jersey City, with bad nights of violence August 2, 3, and 4 in Jersey City.

On one of those days, August 4, the bodies of the Mississippi civil rights workers Goodman, Schwerner, and Chaney, who had been missing for forty-four days, were found in a shallow grave near a farm pond outside of Philadelphia in Neshoba County, Mississippi. Twenty-one white men were arrested in the murder case. When the case was not prosecuted by state, the federal government tried them on civil rights violation charges, and on October 20, 1967—three years later—seven of the twenty-one men were found guilty of conspiracy charges in the slayings by an all-white jury.

A few days after the missing civil rights workers were found, the Monday, August 10, edition of the *Daily News* carried a local story on page one, headlined, "Hooded Men Beat Father, Threaten Son, 12." This was a second incident involving hooded men abducting and beating another white man.

Five hooded men had reportedly taken a Bogalusa area man into the company pasture, beat him with a belt and told his twelve-year-old son he had better not say anything about his father being abducted if he knew what was good for him. They told the boy that they understood that his father had some Negroes at his house playing music with him and that the man had better "straighten up." The beaten man said there was "nothing to it" and that although he and some of his friends had been playing music at the house, they were all white men.

The man's wife told the *Daily News* that she had answered a telephone call about two weeks earlier and had been asked if she and her husband would pay $20 to join a "good organization." She said she told the caller no, they were not interested.

"I used to think maybe there was some good to the Ku Klux Klan," the wife told the paper, "but they're nothing but a pack of no-good devils."

A sighting by a neighborhood youth substantiated the report to the police in every detail.

We addressed the incident the next day, Tuesday, with an editorial that challenged the Klan and their ilk for setting themselves up as the judges of others.

HOW LONG DOES THIS GO ON?

Taking the law into one's own hands is a serious matter, but it is becoming common-place in our area.

A week ago, self-styled guardians of the world's thinking and conduct forced by threats a family to move out of Bogalusa. These people were fine people by every definition of Christian living. They were worth a thousand times the people who threatened them and their family. But their little scheme of hate worked and the family moved away from Bogalusa. It was Bogalusa's loss and it will be marked down as a black day in the records of time for our city.

Two nights ago, a man who lives near Bogalusa and who works in Bogalusa was beaten with a belt in the woods and his 12-year-old son told not to tell about the incident. The child ran home from the incident frightened terribly.

Our self-appointed guardians of all kinds of behavior and morality should take a look at themselves. Unfortunately, they cannot do this objectively. They like themselves and apparently think they are doing the world a favor by keeping everybody else straight . . .

Sooner or later, these kinds of people must be stopped. We, as Americans, must face up to the fact that we live in a democracy and our people are not to be intimidated by hooded saviors of the world. Who appointed these men as our guardians? Are they so holy that they exercise the divine right of judgment of human beings?

It is long past time that our people—you, as Americans—realize that these people have assumed for themselves the rights held only by legally constituted authority and God.

The same day, August 11, authorities said one of three musicians who had gone to the man's house to play music had also told them that there had not been any Black people at the jam session. He also reportedly put in a good word for the Klan to the police, telling them that its members were "God-fearing men" and that the Klan is a "decent organization." He said it was up to the Klan to "rise up and help catch these yellow thugs" who were responsible for the beating and damaging the reputation of the Ku Klux Klan.

Arrest warrants had reportedly been issued for six or seven men believed to be involved, but this seemed to be one of those incidents that just faded away.

Shortly after the paper's story and the editorial about the incident, the Klan's Midnight Mail was back on the streets.

"No doubt you read about the incident which happened in the Mitch community Sunday, August 9," the throw-away flyer stated, "because the editor of the *Daily News,* who is a dastardly, two-bit little coward, made headlines of it. Yes, this little two-bit editor was trying to mold public opinion against the Ku Klux Klan."

The Klan denied having anything to do with the incident, and went on: "You have read articles in the local newspaper branding the Ku Klux Klan as hate-mongers and masked hoodlums and any other slanderous name that the local low-bred woman chaser of an editor could conjure in his filthy little mind. This little local editor is nothing more than a puppet on a string for a certain fat, shyster lawyer on Columbia Street who thinks that he is a big wheel in Bobby Kennedy's Justice Department."

It closed, "Let the *Bogalusa Daily News* continue dealing with the socialists such as Drew Pearson, the Rockerfellows, Scrantons, Javites,

Humphries and many more left-wing liberals. However, let us get a newspaper in Bogalusa that will print the true facts as they happen, not the slanted and biased views this newspaper now prints."

The case of the abduction and beating in Mitch apparently faded away because of a change of heart by the man's wife. Another Midnight Mail was tossed all over the area about a month later, and carried what it claimed was a letter from the wife:

> The following is a copy of a letter sent to the Ku Klux Klan . . . and was received September 21st, 1964:

> To the ORIGINAL KU KLUX KLAN: I apologize for what was written in the *Bogalusa Daily News* about the KU KLUX KLAN on the day of August 10, 1964. After I got over my hysteria about my husband and son, I then knew it had not been KLANSMEN who abducted my husband. I was raised up to believe in the KU KLUX KLAN and what it stood for. I am proud to know that the KU KLUX KLAN originated in the town of Pulaski, in the state of Tennessee, in the year 1867, by God fearing men. I am proud to know that such God fearing men still exist in our country. I am proud to know that the KU KLUX KLAN did not have anything to do with the irresponsible incident that happened at Mitch. I believe that the KU KLUX KLAN will see that justice is done in this matter.

And that was that. The matter seemed to disappear like a puff of smoke. The case apparently got lost in the system and was not prosecuted.

4

A GUN, A CAMERA, AND A CROSS

1964

The Klan went out in force again the night of Saturday, August 15, plant-ing fiery crosses throughout Bogalusa and south of the city in northern St. Tammany Parish. The eighteen crosses reported burned in the city that night between 10:00 and 10:30 p.m. included ones in front of the *Daily News* in the heart of downtown and on my front lawn in the area known as Forest Hills.

But this cross burning was no surprise to me. I had received a phone call the day before from a local police officer, who said he had been asked by the FBI to forward to me a tip that a cross would be burned on my front lawn at precisely 10:00 p.m. that Saturday night. I never did understand why the police told me about it, yet seemed to do nothing to apprehend the cross-burners.

My next-door neighbors were on vacation at the time and, having had a bellyful of the Ku Klux Klan, I set up a plan for that Saturday night. I asked Bob Lawrence of our news staff if he wanted to get in on the plan. He had guns and I had the newspaper's cameras; on Saturday night, we swapped.

Before the appointed time approached on Saturday night, I parked my car on a gravel parking area out near the street in the corner of the yard in front of the house, in a spot that I usually used for the family's second car. My car was perpendicular to the street, and by crouching down in the back seat on the floor, I had a good view of any passing traffic, both coming and going. Bob Lawrence parked his car the same way in the neighbors' driveway, about seventy-five feet from my car.

The plan was for him to be on the floor of the backseat of his car with me on the back floor of my car. I would have the .38 caliber pistol that he loaned to me, and he would have a flash-equipped camera from the newspaper.

We went out to the cars about 9:30 p.m. and waited for the Klansmen to arrive with the cross at ten o'clock, as the policeman had told me. Shortly before 10:00 p.m., several cars began to pass the house again and again, apparently casing our house before planting their cross. Then, right at ten o'clock, one of the cars slowed down near my driveway and then stopped in the street directly in front of the house. Two men jumped from the car and hauled a five- to six-foot wooden cross from the backseat of their two-door car.

My heart pounded and I found myself not knowing what to do. I wanted to shoot, but I knew I couldn't just shoot a man down without being threatened. So I just watched as one of them struck a match and set the burlap-wrapped cross on fire. As they ran back to the car, I raised my head and lowered the window. Just as the car began pulling away, I fired several shots at it. At that instant Lawrence popped up from the back seat of the other car in the next driveway and took a picture of the fleeing automobile.

And they were gone into the night.

It was a small dark car with the license plate covered. There was something very distinctive about it, though: a small air scoop on the hood of the car at the front.

After the camera film was developed and photo printed in the darkroom at the office, I turned the photo of the escaping car over to the FBI. It didn't take them long to trace the car. They found it at local garage near City Hall that was generally known to be a hangout for some Klansmen.

Two days later I wrote the following editorial for the paper, speculating that sometimes the Klan was burning crosses simply to keep the local situation in a state of tension.

AGITATORS VS. AGITATORS

The Ku Klux Klan has announced its presence again, with the usual trappings of mystery.

When the Klan first planted fiery crosses throughout the Florida Parishes in January, the word was "leaked" that the crosses were set out to let the people know that the Klan had risen. Since then, there has been no doubt in anyone's mind of the Klan's presence, so the same excuse for the cross burnings can hardly apply to the Saturday night escapade.

This leaves the one obvious motive—threats of future violence if the population as a whole doesn't toe the Klan's mark.

There has been much justified criticism of Negro agitators who go looking for racial incidents, seeking to trigger violence so that they can persuade the Negro population as a whole that counter-violence is the only means to gain the end they seek.

The Klan seems to be choosing the same route: planting crosses often where no racial trouble has occurred; seeking to keep race relations at the boiling point so that there can be no question of a peaceful solution.

The saddest factor is the sacrilege of the fiery cross itself—the symbol of Christ's sacrifice to bring peace to men, of good will, set afire to serve as a symbol of terrorism.

By this time, the town and parish were mired in racial turmoil and unrest. Confederate flag license plates were more and more in evidence, on the fronts of plenty of cars but especially on the front of pickup trucks that oftentimes had visible gun racks in the rear window of the cab.

The preceding months-on-end of racial strife, boycott threats, and threats of violence had set the stage for what I still consider to be the most meaningful editorial I ever wrote. Looking back, I might confess that it was overly long, but I had a lot to say at the time. What it boiled down to was this: that legitimate political conservatism in the age of US Senator Barry Goldwater was being distorted by hatred and bigotry, and questioning the very need for a hatred-based organization such as the Ku Klux Klan.

I ran it across the bottom of page one of the Sunday, September 6, 1964, edition, and it covered more than one-third of the entire front page "below the fold." The key points were these:

AN EDITORIAL FOR ALL AMERICANS

The people of the United States of America today, as in possibly no other period of this land's history, face a present of unrest and a future of uncertainty. There is on the horizon of this great nation a queue of problems which seem insurmountable. Americans today fight Americans and for many of the same reasons that man has fought man since the Creation by God.

Today, in our small dot on the globe—the dot of Bogalusa, Louisiana, and in our parish—our people face a serious problem. We face the problem of man against man, neighbor against neighbor, friend against friend . . .

We read each day in thousands upon thousands of words in articles and periodicals of the choice which will face the voters of this land in the coming November presidential election. We read of liberals, conservatives, extremists, right-wingers, left-wingers, fellow-travelers, Marxists, Communists, Birchers, Klansmen, racial agitators, demonstrators, Constitutionalists, do-gooders, Fair Dealers, New Dealers, progressives, mainstreamers, middle of-the-roaders and enough more descriptive expressions to fill this and many more pages . . .

We have heard the hue and cry of late primarily of two terms: liberalism and conservatism. Liberalism today in American politics is personified by the President of the United States, Lyndon B. Johnson of Texas. Conservatism is personified by Sen. Barry M. Goldwater of Arizona, himself a candidate for president of the United States . . .

But somewhere along the line, the ugly head of extreme prejudice reared its head. The campaign for, and passage of, the Civil Rights law in the United States Congress, brought about a sudden resurgence of

organizations who confused conservatism and constitutional government with terror, threats, and violence.

In view of this legal and very much American right to organize and
do political battle, where lies the necessity for an organization such as
the Ku Klux Klan? Its members claim that they are God-fearing members of society who are dedicated to the preservation of constitutional
government . . .

We have seen some of our citizens beaten; we have seen some of
them threatened; we have seen some of them ridiculed. We have seen
the Ku Klux Klan in action at night, burning crosses, attempting to put
fear into our people. We have seen neighbor turn against neighbor;
friend against friend, American against American. This is not for the
good of our country, it is not for the good of our people, it is not for the
good of our small dot on the globe . . .

Some of the more radical leadership of the Ku Klux Klan may tell
its followers that this person or that person is a "red" or a "commie" or
an agitator. Words and terms are loosely thrown about and some of our
most dedicated American citizens are reviled among man—all because
they do not share the same views as others . . .

We ask every father of little children, every husband, every mother,
to consider thoughtfully and with Christian conscience the fact there is
no need for the strife which is on the verge of dividing our city. Members of the Ku Klux Klan who believe in their cause and in their quest
for constitutional government can best serve their cause—and America's—by removing the cloak and hood and working for their belief in
the light of day as law-abiding American citizens.

That particular editorial had the local KKK hopping mad. The Klan's
writer of their Midnight Mail must have immediately taken to his type-
writer to fire back, because the sidewalks and driveways around the
city were littered with the rolled-up, rubber-banded sheets only a few
nights after my September 6 editorial. It offered justification for its
secret membership and their use of the hood, and then struck out in

retaliation at all of the favorite Klan targets. It even took a shot at the writer of a letter to the editor that came out in the paper following the previous Midnight Mail.

That writer had written that,

It becomes evident, then, that the success of this group comes solely from the appeals of prejudice to a group of deeply prejudiced people. Like many other such inflammatory groups, the appeal of strong, ugly mud-slinging language is necessary to lead a people who must feel a basic guilt, to believe that they are right. . . . A hate object is always a necessity, and in this case the victim is a man who has the sheer nerve to speak in peril to his life and safety and those of his loved ones. . . . Deny it as they will, the Klan members are hate-mongers who, no matter how hard they try to be non-violent (which, granted, some KKK leaders have tried to be) are going to cause by their very nature, violence and unhappiness.

In late September, I received another letter from the woman in Varnado who, after urging me earlier in the year to be cautious and not cross the Klan, had occasionally written other letters to the editor that were published. But most recently she had sent some writings focused on communism that the paper had not run, and her newest letter accused Bascom Talley of censoring the paper's contents and it mentioned seeing his name in the anticommunist publication The *Councilor*.

I wrote her back that,

Mr. Talley was not even aware that you had written any such articles and is too busy to be bothered with reading and screening letters which come to the *Daily News*. I am the editor and publisher of the *Daily News* and I make the decisions on what goes into the paper and what does not. . . . You will think what you like about the exercise of editorial policy at this newspaper. I am sure that there is no convincing you or any of the other misinformed people in this matter. But that is of no concern to me.

I also told her that, "Knowing *The Councilor* for what it is, it's certainly a pity that a man of Mr. Talley's high character ever had to be subjected to having his name in such a publication."

I had copied the letter to Talley, and he sent me a handwritten note:

> Every so often in life something really nice happens—your letter was one of those things. I appreciated your defense of me more than you know—even though it may subject you to additional diatribes from the bigots or the uninformed. I have often said that you only make a few real friends in this life. I am proud to have you as one.

In early October, an incident on Columbia Street involved a group of white teenagers in a car harassing some Black men who were riding along in a pickup truck, minding their own business. And in the October 5 edition, what might have been a short news story was instead the subject of an editorial:

DISRESPECT FOR THE LAW

There are hundreds of thousands of laws in this land, written down for all men to obey in order to keep the peace.

Friday night in Bogalusa, on Columbia Street, there was evidence of the moral law of man being broken. There was a small white car in which there were six young boys, all of whom appeared to be in their teens. The car had a Mississippi license plate.

Driving along in front of this car was a pickup truck. Inside the cab were two Negro adults. Sitting in the rear of the pickup truck, on the side of the body facing toward the inside, was another Negro adult, a man.

Suddenly, the small white car zipped out of its lane and passed the truck on the right side. As the car passed the truck, the youth in the left rear seat of the car leaned far out the window of the car and slapped at the Negro man sitting in the rear of the truck.

How can we ever expect to live in peace in our land with such obvious expressions of racial hatred displayed in our midst? The untiring efforts of so many people to promote peace and harmony can suffer immeasurably by the reckless acts of hatred on the part of a few. Both races have been guilty of senseless things such as this. As pointed out by FBI Director J. Edgar Hoover, there has been a growing disrespect for the law, which his now famous report stated was the cause for the racial riots in the north and east not long ago.

Both races in these wearying times must face up to their responsibilities to work at preserving the peace and finding it in their hearts to put into daily practice the Golden Rule.

5

THE KLAN WINS A ROUND

1964–1965

Tension continued in the town during those autumn days of 1964, but nobody had any idea that the "Brooks Hays period" of the upcoming winter would turn out to be so hate-filled and full of danger.

Early in December, a group which would shortly become rather infamous in Bogalusa met at the home of Bascom Talley, who had been named a local liaison with the US Department of Commerce's Community Relations Service. I was among those gathering. The topic at hand was an invitation to former Arkansas Congressman Brooks Hays to come to Bogalusa and speak to a public meeting on how the community might avoid further racial strife. Representative Hays, a former president of the Southern Baptist Convention, was nationally recognized as a racial moderate who felt it was much more advantageous to work through racial differences with cooperation rather than confrontation.

It was just that simple an idea. He was not being invited to promote integration, fight segregation, or espouse any other "-ation" of the times—as the Klan would soon charge.

Much of what we discussed at Talley's home that night centered more on who would be personally invited to the public meeting. It did not occur to our group that the mere invitation to hear Congressman Hays speak would produce such a firestorm in the town.

The group gathered with Talley and myself included Reverend H. Bruce Shepherd, the rector at the St. Matthew's Episcopal Church; Reverend Jerry Chance, pastor of the Main Street Baptist Church; Reverend

Paul G. Gillespie, pastor of the Memorial Baptist Church; and Ralph Blumberg, owner of local radio station WBOX.

Reverend James Harris, pastor of the ESM Methodist Church, had attended this first gathering of the "Hays Group," but he did not continue his participation after that, so we were the "Committee of Six."

Vertrees Young, highly respected former resident manager of the local paper mill—the engine of the local economy—did not attend the meeting, but he was originally scheduled to be the Master of Ceremonies for program at which Representative Hays would speak. However, even when the meeting was still being planned that had somehow changed.

Prior to any public announcement, we felt that we had to at least run this idea past Mayor Jesse H. Cutrer Jr. to be sure that what we were thinking of doing would not be battled by the city administration. We knew there was no way to keep our intentions fully under wraps until we could publicly announce the meeting with Representative Hays, so we knew we had to let the mayor know of our plan.

So we met with Mayor Cutrer in his office, with Blumberg acting as the group's spokesman, knowing full well that such a group would be seen entering his office though the lobby at City Hall. After he heard Blumberg's pitch of the proposal on our behalf, Cutrer told us he would discuss the matter with the members of the city's governing Commission Council to see what their position would be on an invitation to Representative Hays to speak in the city. We wanted Cutrer to tell us that the city and the council would not fight us on this meeting—that was all we could hope for. Cutrer told us he certainly wouldn't fight it but clearly indicated that it was our initiative and he would not be joining in.

A few days later, on December 11, 1964, the results of his meeting with the council members came in a telephone call from Cutrer to Talley. Talley told me that Cutrer and the council had decided to not be a part of the initiative, but they hoped it would work out well and benefit the community. Cutrer said the city leaders wouldn't oppose having Hays in to speak but were concerned about the repercussions of negative backlash in the community. And Cutrer had taken that stance even before he actually met with a group of 150 hooded Klansmen gathered at the local Disabled American Veterans hall on December 18 to try to cool down the situation in town.

When we found out we would have no resistance from the mayor and council, the group started working on a list of people who would be invited to the Hays meeting. We wanted it to include the city's "movers and shakers": the city's elected leaders, church leaders, educational leaders, doctors, attorneys, and business people—everybody with money, power, and/or influence.

And that would just be the "white" list. Talley, who had connections within the Black community, would come up with a list of similarly influential Black Bogalusans who would also be invited. But the lists were never fully formulated, as the prospects for even holding the meeting began to dim rapidly as soon as it was announced in the December 27 edition of the *Daily News* that Hays had been invited.

If for no other reason, I wish the meeting had happened because it would have been fascinating to see who among the invitees would have had the courage to attend in the face of the Klan's vocal opposition and threats. But I already knew the answer as far as the city leaders were concerned.

In the week following the announcement of the meeting, which was scheduled for Thursday January 7, 1965, the Brooks Hays episode became one of Bogalusa's ugliest.

The members of the Commission Council, who had earlier taken a position of no opposition, were now indicating that they did not think the meeting would serve any good purpose and told the mayor they would not attend. What reportedly concerned them more than anything was that it was to be a "mixed" meeting, with Blacks and whites meeting together.

Councilmen serving at the time were Jimmie Talbot, Marshall Holloway, Arnold Spiers, and Andy Overton. None of these men were openly associated with the Klan or any other kind of hate group. They were moderate men serving in public office in very difficult and dangerous times in the heart of the Deep South. Having known them all, I feel certain that their lack of zeal for such a meeting stemmed from the fact that they did not want to see any further racial confrontations in the city.

On December 29, two days after the announcement of the Brooks Hays meeting in the paper, the Klan again hit the streets with the Midnight Mail, and the diatribe was the Klan's most vile offering yet. In addition to naming the members of the Committee of Six, it outlined and discussed the Klan's perspective on three points: (1) "this meeting of January 7, 1965, is to be an integrated meeting," (2) "this integrated meeting is for the sole purpose of planning the integration of your Churches, Schools, Businesses, Restaurants, Hotels, etc.," and (3) "the *Bogalusa Daily News* did not tell you the whole truth about Brooks Hays. He is a traitor to the South."

And it closed with this warning to the public: "Being a secret organization, we have KLAN members in every conceivable business in this area. We will know the names of all who are invited to the Brooks Hays meeting and we will know who did and did not attend this meeting . . . Those who attend will be tagged as integrationists and will be dealt with accordingly by the Knights of the Ku Klux Klan."

If the Klan had members in "every conceivable business," then how many Klansmen were there in Bogalusa and Washington Parish? No one except the KKK itself knew for sure, but Mayor Cutrer told the *Wall Street Journal*'s Fred L. Zimmerman in an interview at the time, "I've heard estimates of 600 to 1,400. I'd assume it's less than 1,000."

In the same April 1, 1965, *Journal* story, a local businessman told Zimmerman, "It's a shame, but people can't speak their minds freely in Bogalusa today. . . . The difficulty is that nobody knows for sure who's in the Klan."

I wondered to myself if any of the *Daily News* staffers might be members or sympathizers.

At the bottom of that Midnight Mail was a poem penned by one of the Klan members:

There is in Bogalusa a man named Talley,
who with a hand pickled committee has planned an integrated rally;

This man would love the nigger,
in order to grow financially bigger.
He and his committee have come up with an integration plan,
which is bitterly opposed by the KU KLUX KLAN;
Talley has attended Nigger Churches to sing,
this was done to please Martin Luther King;
While Talley sings with his nigger group,
the KU KLUX KLAN will more Knights recruit;
Soon Talley and his committee will know who is boss,
as the KU KLUX KLAN lights the fiery cross.

The next afternoon, on Wednesday, December 30, the governing Vestry of St. Matthew's Episcopal Church, where the Hays meeting was to be held, voted 7–1 against allowing use of the church's Parish Hall—a lovely venue with a high vaulted ceiling that was often used for concerts, plays, programs, and other gatherings—to be used for Hays to speak. The Vestry said that it had not been aware of the purpose of the meeting. However, church's standard procedures allowed the priest to grant use of the building without Vestry approval, and Reverend Shepherd said the meeting could be held there, the Vestry vote notwithstanding.

Fear ran through the city as a result of the Klan's threats against those who might attend the meeting. Reverend Shepherd received phone calls that the Parish Hall would be bombed if the meeting were held.

We began to hear a lot of excuses from people who were being invited to attend. The Hays Committee of Six met and decided that, in the interest of safety to Congressman Hays and to all those who might attend, it made sense to cancel the meeting. Proceeding with the meeting would have subjected everybody to possible serious injury or even death should the Klan actually carry through with its bombing threat.

Moving the meeting to the relatively small but stately courtroom in City Hall was discussed, but we agreed that was pretty much out of the question because we knew that, given their stance, the Commission Council would not allow use of the building for that purpose.

As the city became frantic over prospects of what might happen on the night of January 7, the Committee of Six drafted a statement announcing cancellation of the Brooks Hays meeting. I published "A Public Statement" at the top of page one two days before the meeting, on the afternoon of Tuesday, January 5,1965:

> This is a statement by some of the people who would like to hear the Hon. Brooks Hays speak in Bogalusa . . . to tell of the experiences of other cities and perhaps by this means help eliminate any possible racial problems in our city. The only purpose in having Mr. Hays come to Bogalusa was to profit by the experiences of other cities and to discuss their problems and solutions.
>
> Here is what happened in our community . . .
>
> Pressures were brought to bear on citizens of Bogalusa. The Ku Klux Klan warned them not to attend; they were threatened by the Klan. A publication of the Original Ku Klux Klan of Louisiana stated: "Those who do attend this meeting will be tagged as intergrationists (sic) and will be dlet (sic) with accordingly by the Knights of the Ku Klux Klan . . . "
>
> Fear continued to grow in our community . . .
>
> It is a shame, and we are ashamed, that fear should so engulf our community that it strangles free speech and the right of peaceful assembly, and makes a mockery of democracy. Do we have a democracy without freedom from fear?

It was signed at the bottom by all of the members of the Committee of Six.

. . . .

In the midst of the Brooks Hays furor, after the announcement of the Hays meeting but before it was scheduled to happen, another round of cross burnings took place in the city. It was on the night of Thursday, December 31, 1964—New Year's Eve.

Had the Klan known what was going on inside my house, they might have wanted to resort to something a lot more intimidating than a fiery cross. They had already burned two on my front lawn, as well as one in front of the newspaper's office; so another burning cross brought little fear to me or my family at that point. My oldest son Lou Jr. told me that he and one of Bascom Talley's sons had a friendly boasting competition about which family—the Majors or the Talleys—had had the most crosses burned on their front lawn at any given point in time. I'm not sure which family eventually "won" that honor.

We were having a New Year's Eve party at the house with a small gathering of close friends. When the group noticed the glow from the burning cross on the front window curtains, I pulled them open so we could all have a better look.

My son, Steven, had seen the pickup truck drive off. He said one man was driving and one was in the back of the truck, which he said was red. Everybody went outside to take a look and there was general amusement, with our friends complimenting Peg and I, tongue-in-cheek, that we really knew how to provide unusual party entertainment. And when a late-arriving couple made it, we offered to go outside and relight the cross so they could share in the fun.

But because we had guests, my wife and children weren't able to repeat the fun they had when we got our second cross. On that previous occasion, Peggy had taken action to lessen any fear the kids might be feeling at the ominous sight of a six-foot cross burning in the night on the front lawn. She made it fun for them instead of fearful.

With some untwisted coat hangers and a bag of marshmallows in hand, she took the kids outside for a nighttime marshmallow roast. What must people driving by on Camellia Road—perhaps even the Klan cross burners themselves if they had circled around the block to pass by and admire their handiwork—have thought at the sight of a family of kids laughing in the night while holding out marshmallows to roast on the flames of a burning cross?

Regarding the possibility of the KKK nightriders admiring their "handiwork" that New Year's Eve night, well, there wasn't as much of it—handiwork, that is—as there had been previously. The four crosses burned on our front lawn during that period showed a steady decline in craftsmanship.

The first cross, part of the batch that was spread across the Florida Parishes from Bogalusa to Baton Rouge, was nicely executed as crosses go. The two-by-four boards were properly cut and jointed where the cross's horizontal crossbar met the longer upright portion, and bolted in the center. That batch of crosses may have been soaked in gasoline or some other combustible liquid because it burned for a good while.

The second cross a few months later—the marshmallow cross—was sturdy enough, but the crossbar was nailed to the upright without the nice center joinery. The third cross on New Year's Eve wasn't even nailed—the crossbar was joined to the upright with wire wrapping. The second and third crosses burned well enough with their gasoline soaked burlap wrapping, though.

But the fourth cross. . . . Well, the guy in charge of cross quality control for the local Klan Klavern must have missed that work session, because the horizontal bar was attached to the upright at the center with a wrapping of accelerant-soaked burlap, but no nails or wire. So as soon as the burlap burned through the cross fell apart, with the crossbar falling to the ground.

In retrospect, it was as if the declining quality of cross construction was, somehow, a parallel to what would become the declining influence of the Ku Klux Klan through that period.

The next morning after the New Year's Eve cross burning, I hauled the charred cross into the back yard and planted it beside the patio, next to the first two crosses.

The same day, on New Year's Day of 1965, Council Commissioner Spiers, who oversaw the Police Department, announced that his department was offering a $500 reward for information leading to the arrest and conviction of anyone who had burned crosses in Bogalusa on public or private property.

Was it mere coincidence that a reward was offered this time and not for any of the earlier burnings? Was it also coincidence that this time one of the crosses had been burned on the front lawn of a Crown Zellerbach official, where Spiers had his "day-job"? But fat chance that anybody was going to rat on the Klansmen who burned the crosses for a measly $500.

That was all during that same weekend that the upcoming Brooks Hays meeting was uppermost in everybody's mind. On Wednesday, January 6, the day following the notice of cancellation of Hays's appearance, which was to be the next night, we carried a brief statement by Hays, headlined "Brooks Hays Disappointed." The former congressman and then-Rutgers University professor said that while he was disappointed in not being able to share his message of moderation in Bogalusa, his feelings were "nothing compared to the tragedy of a town in the grip of the Ku Klux Klan." Hays said that he was ready to come to Bogalusa "no matter what, and that my wife was spunky enough to come with me. It was their (the committee's) decision. They didn't want to risk it."

He called the Ku Klux Klan "a malignancy . . . which would be bound to fade as others have when good people band together to rid their communities of bigotry and intolerance."

The statement was on page one, and this accompanying editorial was on page 4:

AND SO, THE MEETING IS OFF

A meeting to which leading citizens of Bogalusa would be invited here Thursday night has been called off. Brooks Hays was to be the speaker.

All kinds of conclusions were reached about the meeting, principally by the uninformed and by those unwilling to recognize or accept the true purpose of the meeting . . .

A group of local men thought that Brooks Hays might be able to help our community. He was coming to make a talk to our people. He was not coming to shove anything down anybody's throat. His purpose in coming was to help us. He was to tell us of the experiences of such cities as Little Rock, McComb, Birmingham, Montgomery, Monroe and Hammond. He would tell us what was done to prevent racial demonstrations and violence in some areas. Hays is an amusing speaker and one of the most highly respected of all Baptist laymen.

There are those in our community who were opposed to the Thursday meeting, for various reasons. There would have been some of our responsible Negro leaders invited to this meeting to hear Hays. The racial problem is that of the white people and the colored people—all of our people as a whole. If Hays could have offered us some sound thoughts on helping to solve our problems, we needed our Negro leadership present as well as the white leadership. This is everybody's problem . . .

Threats were made repeatedly against the men who set up this meeting. The Ku Klux Klan made a bold blanket threat against anyone who attended the meeting. As free American citizens, it was our hope that every Bogalusan invited to this meeting would stand up for his right to attend a meeting. Those fighting the meeting in various ways would have had you believe that those who attend the meeting were "intergrationists" (sic). Nothing could be more ridiculous. It was to have been a meeting at which a great American and great Baptist layman would speak to us and attempt to help us. After all, this is America, not Castro's Cuba, Hitler's Germany, or the Ku Klux Klan's world. But we must go on—and hope.

And that was it. It was a "done deal." There was no community meeting with Hays, and the Ku Klux Klan had won that round.

Not surprisingly, Governor John McKeithen said in a news conference that same day, "If I were Brooks Hays, I would stay in Arkansas. They have had twice as much trouble as we have had." Hays said he would comply with the governor's wishes, but he said it was the "first time in my long history of visits that any responsible official has intimated that I would not be welcome."

Mayor Cutrer had his say, too. He went on the local radio station the day after the cancellation and said the publicity surrounding the Hays meeting had hurt the city's image. He even told the United Press International that he and the council had tried to keep his radio statement address confined within the city because he didn't want any more bad publicity. It was at that point that we in the Committee of Six realized that the general feeling of the mayor and the council was that we had done something very wrong in inviting Hays.

It all turned out just as Talley had prophesied in a December 11 phone call with Mayor Cutrer: ". . . You will be in a position to cash in or deny it, whichever is best, because if it goes well, fine; and if not you fellows have no connection with it." It surely didn't go well, and the city fathers surely did distance themselves from any connection to the event.

UPI reported that "the mayor, council and city attorney (Robert Rester) complained the Hays incident had led to 'unfair and untrue criticism' of the city and its people. But they said they want everyone to know that they stand firmly for enforcement of all laws, city, state and federal."

"We are unalterably opposed to violence in any form or fashion at any time," read the joint mayor-council statement to UPI. "We will use the full force and effect of the law to prevent it or bring to justice those who perpetrate it." But the mayor and council members didn't see fit to specifically call out the Klan in their opposition to violence; they were more focused on the bad publicity the city was getting.

In a comment to a *Wall Street Journal* reporter a few weeks later, an unnamed local resident may have spoken more truth than many in the city cared to admit: "The good people of this town may not like the Klan, but they like the idea of integration even less. So they're willing to look the other way and let the Klan do their dirty work."

A week after the Hays talk was canceled and after Governor McKeithen had suggested that Hays "stay in Arkansas," the Catholic newspaper in New Orleans, the *CLARION Herald*, commented on the matter and the situation in Bogalusa, headlining an editorial in its January 14 edition: "Who is the real boss?"

The editorial noted Cutrer's and the Commission Council's refusal of use of the City Hall Courtroom for the Hays meeting, and Governor McKeithen's lack of condemnation of the Klan in Bogalusa for its successful campaign to kill the meeting with threats to the meetings planners and anyone else who attended.

After coupling the Hays incident with Governor McKeithen's comment of January 7—the very date that the Hays meeting was supposed to have happened—that Louisianians were no longer scared of the Ku Klux Klan and its cross burnings, the editorial closed by restating its headline: "Well, who is boss?"

Soon after, the CLARION Herald received a letter to the editor challenging its editorial. The letter was from Robert "Bob" Landry, who had a long history in local newspapering and was then the editor of the *St. Tammany Farmer*, a weekly newspaper in Covington in neighboring St. Tammany Parish. But Landry lived in Bogalusa.

"Your story titled 'Who is the Real Boss,' issue of January 14, is largely misleading," Landry's letter opened. Landry asserted that ". . . thus far, no news media has had the truth, nor have they seemed interested in the truth."

Defending the church leadership that had voted to block the use of the Parish Hall for the Hays meeting at St. Matthew's Episcopal, where Landry was a member, Landry said the decision had been made before the Klan's bombing threat had been known. The church hall was no place for a political meeting, the Vestry had ruled.

"News regarding the meeting and the controversy which followed was presented to the public in exceedingly biased fashion, and to this day has never been told in straightforward reporting, as I am now attempting to do," Landry wrote. "The meeting, when made fully known in all its areas, was never popular with the mainstream of Bogalusa."

He closed, "Actually, the entire matter was making a mountain out of a mole hill. Calling Bogalusa 'a city ridden with fear' was not merely a gross exaggeration—it was an untruth. Bogalusa has never had any kind of serious race relations, though such magnification of a story with racial overtones surely could bring trouble to bear."

I was amused when the editors at the CLARION Herald caught an unintended gaffe in that last part of Landry's letter and used it to make a point in the paper's response. Noting Landry's declaration that "Bogalusa has never had any kind of serious race relations," the editors responded, in part, "Editor Landry is more truthful than he realizes . . ." that Bogalusa had never had any kind of serious race relations.

On January 10 came a letter to the editor to the *Daily News* defending the Klan: "Bascom Talley, Lou Major, Ralph Blumberg and a few so-called pastors were surprised to find their little secret for the citizens of Bogalusa out in the open." The writer was apparently referring to the cancelled Brooks Hays appearance, but that was no secret—it had been announced in the paper before it was called off.

"You say that they (the Klan) have spread fear in our community," the writer added, "but be honest with yourself—if they were so cruel and heartless, don't you think Bascom Talley would need another toy to pull along as editor of his cheap lie-printing paper after all the things you have printed about them?"

The writer then dared me to print the letter: "(You) said you would print any letter to the editor signed. Will you print this one praising the K.K.K?," and she signed the letter. I must concede that she showed more bravery in signing her name than other writers of that type of letter (we got one every so often, but they were anonymous), but the *Daily News* did not publish the letter.

A few days later, I was copied on a letter to Reverend Bruce Shepherd from a Tuscaloosa, Alabama, law firm that was representing the *Tuscaloosa News* in a libel suit brought by Robert Shelton, the Imperial Wizard of the United Klans of America. The attorney asked Reverend Shepherd if he would kindly provide copies of the local Midnight Mail and any other threatening material that had been used to force the cancellation of the Hays appearance.

Another newspaper not in the Klan's good graces.

A month later, Bascom Talley gave me a copy of a letter he had sent to Milt Wick, the majority owner of the paper. He was kind enough to open with, "I think Lou Major has done a superlative job recently in a difficult situation," but the letter focused on how Bogalusa's troubles might impact the local economy because they both owned a piece of the *Daily News* and were, of course, interested in its continued profitability.

Talley wrote to Wick, "We may or may not have made a mistake" in inviting Hays into town to speak, "but whether we did or not, someone at some time had to face the Klan issue in Bogalusa." He noted that "Lou has cooperated beautifully with the Mayor and Safety Commissioner by not publicizing racial incidents that would tend to create problems" and added that he thought that Mayor Cutrer and Safety Commissioner Arnold Spiers "are dedicated to preserving law and order in Bogalusa."

Talley closed: "To this point we have only had garbage, phone calls, tacks in the driveways, etc. I'm hopeful that this will be the extent of our difficulty."

6

SWIMMING ACROSS THE OCEAN ALL ALONE

1965

There are times in one's life when he or she feels they are swimming across the ocean all alone, even against a swelling tide. The six men of that Brooks Hays group surely seemed to be swimming out there all—or almost all—alone.

There were precious few people willing to support us publicly. In Bogalusa and Washington Parish, it was clear and simple: they were afraid. I knew there were some people who didn't want to beat Black people or set fire to their homes and churches. There were some who realized the horrible indignities of having to eat only at "colored" restaurants, or to enter the movie theater by a separate entrance and sit upstairs in the movie house so the white people would not have to be near them, or to drink from a water fountain marked "colored," or to sit behind a partition sectioning off the "white only" area at the front of a bus.

But those people were very silent in Bogalusa. They kept their thoughts to themselves.

I did receive some bits of support from out-of-towners, though.

From the Catholic Archdiocese of New Orleans: "Your leadership in the uphill struggle against the Klan is a source of inspiration to all who ply the journalistic profession. The Page 1 statement in your January 5 issue was a masterpiece. The editorial board of the *CLARION* is planning an editorial to support your position."

From the Fellowship of Reconciliation of Nyack, New York: "We join with you in sorrow that the unhealthy force of pressure within your community has prevented the appearance of Brooks Hays. We applaud your courageous gesture in inviting him to speak at the meeting in Bogalusa, and we want you to know that it has not been lost on the rest of the country."

From a writer in Arkansas:

> The sad thing that comes from the recent cancellation of the planned speech or talk in your city by the Hon. Brooks Hays is that all of the ignorance and bigotry that has been centered in our beloved southland is in no place greater than Bogalusa. . . . We hope that your paper will be helpful in educating the people in your community of the changes that are here at hand. Brooks Hays—as fine a man as ever served this country could enlighten your people. WHAT IS WRONG WITH ENLIGHTENMENT?

And while I was surely grateful to get those few words of encouragement, where were the "heavy hitters"?

The Community Relations Service of the US Department of Commerce had had some initial involvement. I knew that Bascom Talley had been at least conferring with them early on in hopes that Bogalusa could avoid racial unrest. Senior Field Conciliator Jerome E. Heilbron and Max Secrest of the department had come to Bogalusa in the latter days of 1964, and it was actually Heilbron who suggested inviting Brooks Hays to speak in Bogalusa. But through it all, when push came to shove, there was no support of any kind from Heilbron or the Community Relations Service.

I had sent copies of all Klan material I had gathered and collected to Heilbron. His response to me on January 13 was:

> Dear Lou:
>
> Enclosed are all copies of the news items and other documents you sent me relative to Klan activities in the Bogalusa area. Thank you very much for furnishing this information to me.
>
> Best personal regards,
> Jerry

That was it. Nothing about the cancelled Hays meeting that Heilbron himself had suggested. Not even an "attaboy" to the *Daily News*. I never heard from Heilbron or anybody at the CRS again.

In mid-January came two separate personal notes of support from Rosemary Wick, wife of Milt Wick. My wife Peggy received the first one, which simply offered moral support. In mine, which came a few days later, Mrs. Wick told me that she had read the page one statement about the cancellation of the Hays meeting. In those days before the internet, Milt Wick or someone else at the Wick offices in Arizona would have had to bring a copy of that issue of the *Daily News* to Mrs. Wick at her home for her to read it. It was interesting to know that the goings-on in Bogalusa were being talked about at the Wick household in the Phoenix, Arizona, suburb of Scottsdale.

After the announcement and subsequent cancellation of Hays's appearance in town, a concerted drive was launched against the newspaper in mid-January and it continued for more than two months. There was an active telephone campaign to get subscribers to cancel their *Daily News* subscriptions. The effort was having an effect: we were getting "stops" at the rate of ten to fifteen a day—sometimes more, sometimes less.

Fear played as much a part in it as did dedication to the Klan or its cause. We knew this was true because many people told our office clerks that they had been "warned" to stop taking the *Daily News*. They said they had no choice, some apologized, some said they might start back later.

A local paper mill worker told Circulation Manager Harold Jung that talk was going around the mill for people to quit the paper; mill workers were being told the *Daily News* was trying to push integration. On Saturday, January 23, we had a record forty-two stops called in by readers. The figures proved how effective the scare tactics were. Our paid circulation went from 8,500 to 7,500 in a little over two months. We did note some corresponding increase in news rack sales, but nothing to equal the drop in home delivery.

The "anti-" circulation campaign was accompanied by an assortment of other forms of harassment aimed at the newspaper and at me and my family.

One night in mid-January, two of our newspaper vending racks were stolen at the eastern fringe of our circulation area across the Pearl River in Mississippi. A rack had also been stolen the week before in Bogalusa. No other newspapers' machines, usually lined up next to ours at the same stores, were stolen.

We began getting complaints of papers not being delivered. Our carriers assured us they were delivering them, which meant somebody was following the carriers and picking them up before the subscribers could get them from their front sidewalk or driveway.

On that same Sunday morning in January when the boxes were stolen in Mississippi, eight bundles of our papers were dumped at the front of the *Daily News* office. They had been "spotted" to our carriers' front doorsteps after the Saturday midnight pressrun for home delivery on Sunday morning. Someone had followed behind, picked up the bundles before the carriers woke up, and brought them back to dump at the office side door into the Circulation Department. The bundles, each marked with the paper route number and number of papers for delivery, were redelivered to the carriers, so the only effect was the minor inconvenience of a later delivery for subscribers on those routes.

During that week, a dead dog was thrown on my lawn, a bag of shrimp peels and crab shells was scattered in my driveway, and an egg was thrown against the door of the Circulation Department at the paper. Other nights during that troubled period, our yard was "rolled" with toilet paper, and once someone even scattered dozens of outdated posters, left over from a recent area rodeo, across the lawn.

On Thursday, January 28, the manager of a loan company whose office was around the corner from the newspaper told me about a meeting of about ten people that had been held several days earlier by a group talking about starting another newspaper in Bogalusa. A newsprint salesman had met with the group, and the startup target date was supposedly March 1, 1965.

Our Advertising Manager Harry Wilson had heard that the newsprint salesman would be returning for another meeting with backers of the prospective paper. Their group had contacted Wilson, ad salesman Ivy

Cutrer, and Circulation Manager Harold Jung to leave the *Daily News* and go to work for them. I was also told that ad saleswoman Dorothy Seal and pressman "Red" Applewhite were contacted to go to work for them. However, neither of them came and told me that as Harold Wilson, Ivy Cutrer, and Harold Jung had done.

On March 10, I posted a notice on the office Bulletin Board asking for anyone who had been contacted to let me know. Nobody else came forward as Wilson, Cutrer, and Jung had already done. Dorothy Seal had always shown loyalty to the newspaper, so I imagine she did not come forward due to fear.

A few days earlier on Sunday, March 7, a teacher at rural Thomas High School who was known to be involved with the white supremacists in the parish had a housewarming out in the country. Denman Pace, one of our pressmen, told me he had attended the housewarming out in the parish. Pace told me he saw several Bogalusa city officials there, and other known white supremacists from Bogalusa were in attendance. Pace said he had attended because his father lived in the Thomas community and had been invited. Literature was being handed out at the housewarming, but Pace didn't get to see what it was.

At that time, Mayor Cutrer continued to try to shore up the city's image.

On Wednesday, January 27, he had summoned many people into his office to tell them about tests of accommodations that would be made in the following days. He had both the (New Orleans) *Times-Picayune* and (Baton Rouge) *Morning Advocate* reporters in for the briefing, but the *Daily News* was not even told of the meeting. It had become evident by then that Cutrer was playing his cards to show that he was avoiding the *Daily News*—no doubt the aftermath of the Brooks Hays situation. In a radio speech that night, he referred to the "regrettable statement" which appeared in the *Daily News*—the one that I had written announcing the cancellation of the Hays meeting.

He had several meetings in his office that day. The daylong parade into Cutrer's office included owners and operators of some fifteen Bogalusa restaurants and the two movie houses. One of the gatherings in his City Hall office at 5:00 p.m. included the Chamber of Commerce manager, a local pastor who was thought of as being at different ends of the spectrum from Reverends Chance, Gillespie, and Shepherd (of the Hays Group), and an attorney who was among those trying to organize the start-up newspaper.

For some unknown reason, they called Leonard Parker, a *Daily News* pressman, and he had attended the evening gathering in the mayor's office. Parker told me that a local businessman who had also been at the meeting about starting a new newspaper had led a standing ovation for Mayor Cutrer and Safety Commissioner Arnold Spiers, for standing up for Bogalusa amidst all the bad national publicity. Once again, the *Daily News* was not notified or invited to the gathering. And I never could figure out why Parker had not called to tell me about his invitation before the meeting but waited to tell me about it the next day.

The mayor's radio address that night was one of determined moderation and it set a roadmap for peaceful desegregation.

He said of the upcoming restaurant and lunch counter tests: "We feel that every citizen of every race in Bogalusa will be calm, straight-thinking, level-headed and concerned for the best interests of our community and its future. Here in our city, we do not have to go through the same ordeal that has happened in many other cities throughout the nation, and with the help of Almighty God, it will not be so."

He said the tests would provide Bogalusa with an "opportunity to prove beyond a question of a doubt what kind of people we are, and opportunity to display our dignity and character for the whole nation to see, and to prove to those who believe otherwise that we believe in the orderly process, that we uphold and support law and order, that we are opposed to violence and disorder, that all peoples of all races who live here are working together for the best interest of our city."

The mayor introduced Safety Commissioner Arnold Spiers, who made a blunt statement on law and order and what the people could expect from the Bogalusa Police Department. He said police would enforce the law and protect the rights of all citizens. He said law enforcement would "apply equally and without favoritism regardless of race, creed or color. Law enforcement in this city will not break down but will be carried out to the fullest extent."

Spiers got more specific when he said that "sit-downs or other acts that prohibit the safe and peaceful movement of persons and vehicles in the public streets and prevent access to buildings are a violation of law, and any who use these means to gain their ends are subject to arrest." Commissioner Spiers had put on notice anybody who felt they were going to forcefully prevent Blacks, civil rights workers, or anybody else from having full access to local businesses.

Ronnie Moore, the representative for CORE in the Louisiana Sixth Congressional District, had been in Bogalusa for several days, training those who would test the accommodations on January 27. Moore's name became synonymous in Bogalusa with everything hard-core segregationists hated.

When the testing of restaurants, the public library, cafes, and movie houses did occur in early 1965, it all went quietly. Teams of young local Blacks were seated and served without incident. Several received library cards at the Bogalusa branch library. Two Blacks went to each of the two side-by-side movie houses on Columbia Street that evening and had the theaters—downstairs—to themselves, as no whites showed up. They didn't finish the movies, staying for only about twenty minutes before leaving. I don't remember what was playing, but the two people obviously weren't there for the movie.

Assistant Police Chief L. C. Terrell said there was a little bit of heckling at the Redwood Cafe when the testing team left there, but he quieted them down and there was no further incident.

The tests were carried out by members of the Bogalusa Voters League, with two CORE members acting as advisors, according to Voters League President Andrew Moses.

Bill Yates, a white man from Boston, and Steve Miller of San Francisco, both CORE volunteers, kept watch on the day's activities. Mayor Cutrer and the Commission Council members kept up with the events of the day by police radio from City Hall.

One surprise came when the group went to test Woolworth's. They found that the stools had been removed the night before and the lunch counter was shut down. It never reopened. At most of the other restaurants and cafes tested, white patrons left when Blacks sat down and were served.

Nevertheless, Moses said the day had gone well and that everybody in Bogalusa had acted responsibly. Yates, the CORE "watcher" from Boston, said, "Without reservation, if other cities in Louisiana do as well as the civic authorities in Bogalusa, it would be a different place."

Yates said he planned to remain in Bogalusa for several more weeks to make sure things continued to go smoothly, while Miller, the watcher from San Francisco, said he was going to leave the following Friday.

While the testing went calmly, the next week saw another problem arise when Yates and Miller claimed they had been accosted and chased by a group of whites outside a Black neighborhood bar. There were wildly conflicting reports of what did and did not take place. City officials and police said they investigated the report of the attack and found no evidence that it had actually occurred.

At the same time, Voters League President Andrew Moses said he had been promised by CORE official Moore that Yates and Miller would be gone from Bogalusa by that time and would not return. Moses was reportedly angered by the fact that the CORE members were still in town—not only because they were there, but because Moore had told him that they would not be.

Moses said he felt that negotiating with the mayor and townsfolk was preferable to more demonstrations. Moses was a sandwich shop operator who later became an advertising salesman and announcer for radio station WBOX. Some of the more militant activists in the Black community were critical of Moses for his continuing efforts to work with the mayor and the council.

When it was time for Yates and Miller to leave town, they were escorted out of the city by local police and then by state police from the city limits on to Baton Rouge.

At the precise time the testing and discord over CORE's presence in town were taking place, Mayor Cutrer had received a three-page letter from the US Department of Commerce's Community Relations Service, the federal office agency that had earlier given me the cold shoulder. The letter looked at "the big picture" and revealed an interesting behind-the-scenes scenario in Bogalusa.

The letter was written to Mayor Cutrer and copied to all members of the Commission Council, apparently after the mayor had spoken with Associate Director for Conciliation John A. Griffin at the Community Relations Service on February 23, 1965.

Griffin opened the letter by chiding the mayor and Commission Council for, apparently, not following his advice:

> We discussed the fact that Bogalusa is sitting on a dynamite charge, and the fuse is already lighted! This situation arises from various causes. But an immediate cause is the fact that when you planned your testing of public accommodations, you found it convenient to have the assistance of CORE as a sort of stalking horse for this operation. Our suggestion had been that such "testing" be done without publicity, through the quiet, planned, cooperative efforts of Bogalusa citizens, Negro and white. This approach has been followed with success in many other cities in the South. Your choice of a different route really poses some new situations for you.

A possible result, Griffin speculated:

> If your city becomes a focal point for any national group whose policy calls for strong, affirmative action for immediate change—or even if your local Negro citizens get increasingly impatient with the continued denial of their lawful rights—Bogalusa's situation could be more difficult. This is because of the protests of the Klan members and because their successes have surely discouraged them!

And he took the mayor to task for some of the earlier events involving members of the Group of Six that had invited Brooks Hays to speak:

I think that finding some convenient whipping boy for these facts doesn't solve the problem! Running a minister out of town because he sponsors a meeting that never came off certainly doesn't solve the problem. Economic reprisals against the owner of a newspaper or radio station who happens to believe that there has to be some serious discussion of enforcement of the laws of the United States is certainly no solution.

What WERE Griffin's suggested solutions? The business community needed to understand just how much was at stake in the situation. City law enforcement should be stepped up and,

> . . . [W]hites who may be inclined to take the law into their own hands must understand who is in control. The mayor and council have a clearer view of what the local Negro leadership wants by setting up some kind of machinery so that there can be some more certain communication between representatives of the Council and the white leadership and the Negro community. And desegregation of the restaurants, motels and other public accommodations must be achieved.

And Griffin added to the mayor that "I still think Brooks Hays should be invited to Bogalusa. This would do much to increase the respect for your city throughout the Nation. At home it would make clear that you believe in freedom of speech and that you, not the Klan, control your town."

But that surely never came to pass.

Meanwhile, Circulation Manager Harold Jung told me that he had been called again by a member of the group planning to set up another newspaper, asking him to move over to the new paper. Jung told them he was not interested, and he was told he would live to regret it.

Also during that time, Lou Jr., then fourteen years old, was riding his bicycle home from his weekly Saturday morning trip to the *Daily News* circulation office, where he had gone to give Jung the previous evening's weekly subscription payments he had collected along his paper route. On his way back to our home in Forest Hills, he took his standard shortcut route through the woods along the Bogue Lusa Creek behind our home.

In a clearing where numerous trails through those woods converged, he happened upon a gathering of eight teenaged boys, most of whom were his classmates at Bogalusa High School. When he asked them what they were doing, they said they were having a meeting of the "Junior Ku Klux Klan." Lou Jr. continued on his way without incident to our home only two hundred yards away through the woods. Whether or not a true "Junior Klan" existed or those boys merely fancied themselves as members of the KKK, I reported the gathering to the police because it was so near in the woods behind our home.

A few days later, I received a copy of the report from the police investigation into the matter. They had tracked it down. No charges were filed because the boys were just hanging around in woods that had easy public access, and they had not been doing anything illegal. But I was given a list of each boy's name, age, home address, and who his father was—the latter being insightful information. One of those fathers was a well-respected pastor in town. Others worked in the paper mill.

As the *Daily News* editor, Lou Major accepts an
award to the paper from the Louisiana Press
Association in 1961.

CROSS IN LACOMBE —Silhouetted against the sky is one of scores of crosses which were burned across Southeast Louisiana Saturday night in an organized "scare campaign". The cross shown here was burned at an intersection of highways in Lacombe in St. Tammany Parish, identical to crosses found burned in Washington Parish and the other Florida Parishes between 10 p. m. and midnight Saturday. (Staff Photo by Lou Major).

One of the Ku Klux Klan crosses burned across the Florida Parishes in early 1964.

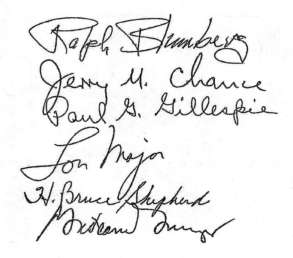

The signatures of the members of the "Committee of Six"
accompanied the Page 1 statement about the cancellation
of Brooks Hays's speaking engagement.

Lou Major fired several shots at this car speeding away after the Klansmen had been lighting a burning cross on the lawn in front of his home.

This photo was the only one of the Black marches that appeared in the
Daily News.

This poster announced a Ku Klux Klan rally the day after Christmas in Bogalusa and the day after that across the Pearl River in Mississippi. Poster in author's collection.

As the Klan days began to cool by the late 1960s, Peggy and Lou Major, *left,* attended a Wick company meeting with Bascom and Imogene Talley.

There was still a Ku Klux Klan in Bogalusa in 1976 when Lodge W-27 of The Invisible Empire Knights of the Ku Klux Klan, Realm of Louisiana, opened a lodge in Bogalusa, complete with a ribbon-cutting by the then-mayor.

7

LEAVE THIS TOWN TO THE DEVIL

1965

In February 1965, local Blacks took a lead from a group in another Louisiana paper mill town, Jonesboro, and established a local chapter of the Deacons for Defense and Justice. Blacks in Jonesboro had organized the Deacons for Defense in November of the previous year, and the Bogalusa chapter formally organized on February 21—the day that Malcolm X, leader of the nation's Black Muslims—was assassinated. Bogalusa's Blacks had decided that it was time to meet the Ku Klux Klan's threats and violence against the Black community with—if necessary—armed resistance.

Founded by Robert Hicks, A. Z. Young, and Charles Sims, who served as president and public spokesman for the group, the Deacons also served as protectors of civil rights workers who visited the city during that period.

The Jonesboro group may have been the first of what would eventually be about twenty chapters and twice that number of "affiliates" in towns across the Deep South and even in Chicago, but the Deacons in Bogalusa were second and arguably the most noted. The 2003 film *Deacons for Defense*, a made-for-TV movie starring Forrest Whitaker, was about the Bogalusa chapter.

As the unrest in the city unfolded in 1965, local Blacks had begun a boycott of white-owned-and-operated businesses in the city because of white indifference to job opportunities for Blacks. Some business people said business was down 20 to 40 percent.

Oddly enough, while the Klan had been working to hurt the paper by trying to convince our subscribers to quit, we were caught up in the Black boycott at the same time.

A Black carrier boy got into an argument out on the street at our Circulation Department when he came to pick up his newspapers for delivery in a Black residential section of town. When he got home, he told his parents that he had been beaten up by a white carrier boy "inside" the newspaper's Circulation Department. Word spread throughout the Black community, and almost overnight several hundred individuals stopped taking the paper.

Harold Jung knew a number of Black ministers and other community leaders, however, and finally the carrier boy told them the truth—that he had gotten into the fight outside of the building and that neither Jung nor other Circulation Department staff knew anything about it until it was all over. The Black residents immediately resumed their subscriptions, but not before some scary incidents took place.

Jung himself, delivering papers in one of the Black residential areas near downtown and our office, had his car almost rolled over by a group who still thought somebody inside the newspaper building had attacked the young carrier.

In response to the problem of some white and Black carrier boys arriving at the same time after school to pick up bundles of papers for their afternoon routes, we started "spotting" the Black carriers' bundles of papers to their homes so they would not have to come to the paper and be confronted by the white boys. Soon after, the white carriers' bundles were also being spotted.

In February, only six weeks after the cancellation of the Brooks Hays talk, one member of the Committee of Six, the Reverend Jerry Chance, was voted out of his position by the members at Main Street Baptist Church. He was given until the end of March to leave. A neighborhood resident and church power broker had been the ringleader in circulating a petition to get rid of Reverend Chance. He preached his farewell sermon in early April. The newspaper the *National Observer* used the event as the lede of a story about Southern racial moderates. In the article, Reverend Chance's only quote was, "In this town, to be quiet on the racial issue is a step toward moderation."

But the article carried a more ominous quote from another Bogalusan. This "prominent" person, who spoke only on an assurance of anonymity, told the *Observer,* "I am fearful that before we are through here there will be bloodshed here. Good friends of mine, people you wouldn't believe it of, are carrying weapons."

In the same *Observer* article, Reverend Paul Gillespie of Memorial Baptist Church and one of the Committee of Six, tried to find the silver lining, telling reporter Jerrold F. Footlick, "We are through as far as influence in the community is concerned. But we have pushed back the walls of extremism on both sides. By committing ourselves, we may have made it possible for others to take moderate positions, to maneuver toward some kind of understanding between the races."

All this time, there was mounting pressure on Reverend Shepherd within his congregation. He told *Wall Street Journal* reporter Fred L. Zimmerman, "The Klan won't be satisfied until we're driven out, but I wouldn't leave this town now." Reverend Gillespie was also coming under pressure at Memorial Baptist by then, and in the same *Journal* story, headlined "Town in Tension," Reverend Gillespie stated, "I'm about ready to leave this town to the Devil."

At about the same time that Reverend Chance was being voted out at Main Street Baptist, the secretary of Reverend Shepherd's Episcopal Church, where I had become a member, refused to include me in the mail-outs of the weekly church bulletin to members of the parish. Reverend Shepherd confronted her about it and she said she would quit her job as secretary before she would mail me the bulletin. He accepted her "resignation" on the spot.

It was also during late January and early February that night-riders undertook a few "tack attacks." All of the Committee of Six members awoke several mornings to find roofing tacks scattered all over the driveways at their homes. I even tried to find out where they had been purchased to see if I might find out who bought them. But the answer was always the same: they were just common roofing tacks that could be bought anywhere.

It fell to my sons to pick up the nails at our house. Collecting them off the cement driveway was easy enough, but more of a challenge was finding them among the small stones of a pea gravel parking pad just off the street beside the driveway, and the Klan was able to claim at least one flat tire for their efforts.

A brick had gouged the front door of our house in February; on another night a headstone stolen from some local cemetery was left on the front doorstep. We never could find out where it came from to return it to its rightful resting place.

The night of Wednesday, February 24, was a scary one. The phone rang and Peg answered it. A man told her she had better leave the house and take the kids with her because "they're going to bomb the house tonight." That's all he said. But he didn't hang up; he left the phone off the hook. I listened and could hear background music and traffic, so it was obviously from an outdoor pay phone someplace. There was no way we could call out for help because the line was kept open by the phone that was still hanging off the hook somewhere in town.

I would not have called the local police, anyhow, because through all of this racial turmoil in the city we had reason to believe that many of the policemen were in sympathy with—if not members of—the Klan. I wasn't going to call in the foxes to come protect my henhouse.

At about the same time, the caller telephoned the home of our next-door neighbor, a local attorney. His wife came over to tell us of the call, which was a warning that our house was going to be bombed. She tried to convince us to leave the house, but I refused to do it. Instead, I went next door and used their phone to call the South Central Bell Telephone Company and ask if they could locate the phone and hang it up. I also asked if they would let me know where it was located. Several hours later, they located the pay phone and cleared our line, but they refused to tell me where it was.

Meanwhile, the neighbors came up with their own solution to our situation. While the phone was still out of service, we ran a string from a window in our house across our two adjoining side yards into a room at the home next door. The string on the neighbors' end had a bell on it; if anything happened and we needed help, we were to pull the string to ring the bell next door. I told the kids in no uncertain terms to not mess with that string.

I turned on the front porch lights, which illuminated the front lawn fairly well, and I got out my shotgun. I got very little sleep that night, staying awake sitting in the dark by the front jalousie window with the loaded gun in my lap, waiting for the KKK's "bomb squad" to show up. We never had to ring the neighbors' bell and I never had to fire the shotgun, because the "bombers" didn't show.

The next morning, I called the telephone company and ordered a new unlisted phone number, and the only people who were given the number were a few trusted people at work and Bascom Talley.

On Tuesday and Wednesday, March 9 and 10, women callers got on the telephone and threatened local businesses with a boycott if they continued to advertise on radio station WBOX, which Ralph Blumberg owned. A good number of the businesses, some national chain stores and other local businesses, did pull their advertising. The manager of one store claimed that the store had seventeen phone calls threatening a boycott of the store within two days, another reported twenty-five calls, and another had eight. The owners of one business told Blumberg of the calls and told him they would stay with him, but Blumberg said he would pull their spots anyway so there would be no trouble for them.

No threatening calls were reportedly made to several Jewish-owned businesses in town; the callers apparently felt the Jewish merchants would stick with the Jewish station owner Blumberg.

As the station battled for survival, Blumberg was ordered to vacate the building he was in by May 31. He moved his station and began broadcasting from a trailer north of town. Most of his advertisers had left him, and donations were actually helping to keep him on the air. When even those dried up, it wasn't long before Blumberg sold the station and moved away from Bogalusa.

We found out that many of the newspaper's advertisers were being called also, but apparently not as many as those of the radio station. We had one advertiser who pulled out—a family-owned neighborhood grocery that never ran ads in the paper again, even after the racial period subsided.

March 1965 was the month of the historic marches from Selma, Alabama, to the state capital in Montgomery that preceded the signing into law of the Voting Rights Act of 1965 by President Lyndon Johnson. There were three marches that month, following the shooting of activist Jimmy Lee Jackson in February by an Alabama state trooper in the nearby town of Marion.

On March 7, marchers in Selma were met at the Dallas County line by billy-club wielding Alabama state troopers, and the "Bloody Sunday" confrontation left sixteen protesters hospitalized and another fifty with lesser injuries. Bloody Sunday was followed on March 9 by "Turnaround Tuesday," when Reverend Martin Luther King Jr. and other marchers turned back when they were not met with any blocking action by state police at the county line. The famed march to the Alabama state capital in Montgomery occurred on March 21–24 and ended with Reverend King asking a crowd of 25,000 from the capitol steps, "How long?" and answering his own rhetorical question with "Not long."

The Selma marches would serve as inspiration for marches two years later in Bogalusa and Washington Parish.

On March 17, 1965, I received a call from newspaper owner Milt Wick. He told me he wanted to see me the next day in Washington, DC, where he would be.

I had an idea what he wanted to see me about, but I wasn't sure. Neither he nor his brother Jim had ever summoned me before. Milt and Jim owned the highly conservative political tabloid newspaper *Human Events.* Milt was president and executive publisher and Jim was editor and operated the influential publication in Washington, DC. They were both politically very conservative and well-connected with the national conservative scene, especially Jim because he lived in Washington.

These were men who were on a first-name basis with Mr. Conservative of America, Senator Barry Goldwater of Arizona.

Jim also shared ownership of the *Daily News* and several other newspapers and was chairman of the newspapers' boards of directors, including that of the *Daily News*. But Jim stayed in Washington and ran *Human Events,* while Milt lived in Arizona and oversaw the brothers' newspapers, including the *Daily News.*

If I wrote that I remember every last detail of that trip to Washington because of its importance in my life, I would be lying. Actually, my mind has found its own way of blocking out almost everything that happened. But I do remember that we met in Milt's hotel room.

And I remember that Milt told me he wanted me to make the *Daily News* a "conservative newspaper." At the time, what seemed strange to me was that I thought I had already done that. If there was anything I did not, and never did consider myself, it was being a "liberal." In fact, I had written an editorial about five months earlier, on October 23, 1964, declaring that the paper was not liberal—or conservative.

LET'S GET THE RECORD STRAIGHT

For some time now, there have been those in and around Bogalusa who have found it advantageous to label the *Bogalusa Daily News* as an ultra-liberal newspaper. The jabs have been repeated, low-down and untrue.

. . . [T]he presentation of both views does not qualify a newspaper as either a liberal or conservative publication—unless it is so labeled by those with ulterior motives. Hundreds of different types of stories, columns, letters, pamphlets, etc. come into every newspaper office regularly . . . It must all be weighed carefully by the standards of fair editorial judgment. Much of the material is, in our opinion, slanted one way or another. Everybody has a point he is trying to get across. One example is a letter received just this week in reply to another Letter to the Editor which appeared recently in the *Daily News*. The letter received this week has not been printed and cannot be printed, for one reason: it is libelous.

Insinuations and accusations that outside influence is imposed on the editorial judgment of the *Daily News* are lies. Editorial judgment of the *Daily News* lies with the names of the persons listed on the masthead of this page in the upper left hand corner. There are those who tell other stories, either for their own political or financial gain. But then there are people who do not recognize the truth when they see it. We are not naïve enough to think that these people will accept what is a fact. Nevertheless, it was time that the record be set straight.

The only two quasi-"liberal" things I had done with the *Daily News* was to discontinue the insanity of printing a second "colored" edition every Friday and restoring the Drew Pearson column, which I felt was in the best interest of the newspaper in my attempts to get more circulation.

I never did think that speaking out against the Ku Klux Klan put me in the liberal stable. That was a moral decision from which I never wavered and never will. The Ku Klux Klan was (is), in my opinion, an organization that espouses racial and anti-Semitic hatred and brutality.

Milt told me he wanted me to begin running a column written by Senator Goldwater in the *Daily News*. I had no problem with that whatsoever. I admired Senator Goldwater and much of the politics for which he stood. I was glad to get it.

The one thing I vividly remember Milt telling me was that members of the Ku Klux Klan might be wrong, but, "It's like a religion to them. It's their religion."

My background of total religious tolerance made this difficult to understand. I was born a Methodist and grew up in the Methodist Church as a youngster. When the family moved to an area of Jefferson Parish where there was no nearby Methodist Church, we joined the local Presbyterian Church. In order for me to get what my parents wanted for me—a solid college-preparatory education—I commuted back into the city to attend and graduate from St. Aloysius, a Roman Catholic high school in New Orleans. That included two bus transfers each way and sitting in on daily classes in the Catholic religion for three years.

Somehow, I impressed the Brothers of the Sacred Heart sufficiently that my favorite teacher, Brother Andre, tried to persuade me to become a Catholic, go to a Catholic university, and become a teaching Brother of the Sacred Heart. At the age of sixteen, this scared me more than it flattered me and I entertained no such notion.

And upon arriving in Bogalusa I was an active member of its First Presbyterian Church until I moved to the Episcopal Church because of what I felt were more humanitarian views about those who could and could not enter the House of the Lord.

So when Milt Wick told me that the Klan's precepts constituted their religion, I understood what he was saying to me, even though I shared none of their views and I would never accept the premise that the Ku Klux Klan was a religion.

I left Washington the day after I arrived. I felt, flying back to my little town in Louisiana's deep pine forests, that I had been dutifully spanked, and I still detested the Ku Klux Klan.

Milt was very much a "bottom-liner," and I know he and his brother Jim were concerned with our drop in circulation. They didn't want to see further erosion anymore than I did. They were the paper's owners, but they acted more like coaches, and they gave me the best advice that made sense to them at the time and then sent me back into the game to keep quarterbacking.

While the city's Blacks continued to boycott white-owned businesses, the whites were boycotting a local oil distributor because it had a "colored" service station that was located on a lot owned by Bascom Talley.

As the Wick brothers were my coaches during those winter–spring days of 1965, I was at the same time playing the role of coach and cheerleader for the *Daily News* staff. One of my office bulletin board pieces, which was needed at the time, read, in part:

> It's no secret that there's been talk around our town about boycotting the *Daily News*. Thus far it hasn't had much effect. We have lost some circulation, but a very small percentage. There might be a few advertisers who are a little bit afraid at this point.

But we must move forward. There is no reason for discouragement. We are concentrating on putting out a better newspaper than ever. The News Dept. should look for every opportunity for local news, feature stories, pictures—don't be afraid to write a good story about people and things. Look for them. Let's look around and come up with some good solid features with pictures. These are good interest-builders.

To the Advertising Dept.: stick with it. Make your calls regularly and frequently. Don't pull back. Keep your head high. Nobody in this organization has a thing in the world to be ashamed of. If anybody does feel ashamed to be working for this newspaper, in that frame of mind they would be better off working somewhere else. Reports keep coming back that there are people here who "carry the word" to outsiders of what's going on inside the *Daily News*. I sincerely hope this is not so. But at the same time, we have nothing to hide. The circulation stops have ceased as of today, Friday. Business is holding up, with a few minor exceptions . . .

Let's keep our shoulders to the wheel and get over this hill. We can do it by all working together as we always have. One day, the full truth and its results will be known. At this point, there is no reason to muddy the waters. We all have a job to do. We have more news and pictures to get, we have to work on our advertising as never before, we have to fight for every subscriber. In our little way, we have our basic freedom to preserve—the freedom of the press, for which we all work. Let's take each day one by one and make each day's paper a new testimonial to our very best efforts.

At the same time, the Vietnam War continued to rage and the Black voter registration effort was intensifying in Selma, Alabama. James Farmer, national director of CORE, had labeled Bogalusa and Jonesboro in north central Louisiana as the next "major project," drawing national publicity by making his declaration on ABC television.

On March 16, 1965, Frank M. Johnson Jr., a federal court judge for the Middle District of Alabama, approved plans for the March 21 Selma-to-Montgomery march of Black citizens, led by Reverend Martin Luther King Jr.

A few days after the judge's ruling on the Selma march, Bogalusa Mayor Cutrer called for "civic responsibility" by city and area residents should CORE return to the streets of Bogalusa.

He also named a "Community Affairs Committee" for the city, with local attorney John Gallaspy as chairman. To nobody's surprise, the 24-member committee was made up only of white men. No Blacks, no women, and no local newspaper publisher Lou Major to be sure.

Despite that obvious shortcoming, the paper supported the idea in a March 30 editorial because, well, at least it was something.

COMMITTEE IDEA SOUND

Formation of a Community Affairs Committee in Bogalusa, which will work with city government and with the people of the community, is a good idea.

The purpose of the committee is to help our city and our people. Bogalusa wants no trouble. Our town has its problems, certainly, just as any other town has, whether it be in the North, South, East or West. It is certainly not fair for any town or community to be singled out as a "target area . . . "

Many of the city's finest and most dedicated citizens have responded to the call for membership and are sitting and working on the group's plans for the future. They will work as a team and will meet with our city government leaders to talk over projected plans of action—all designed to preserve the peace in Bogalusa and help in finding solutions to all problems.

This is potentially a great step forward for our community. The members will be wrestling with some tough problems. They should be given encouragement by their fellow Bogalusa citizens in the hope that their efforts will achieve full success.

Bascom Talley had suggested a similar committee—to include Blacks AND whites—two years earlier. In June 1963 he wrote to the mayor asking, "I would like to respectfully suggest Your Honor and the Commissioners (of the city's governing Commission Council) consider the appointment of a committee where-in Negroes would be represented, and thereby keep a direct line open between our City Government and the Negro community."

In his letter of response, Cutrer told Talley that he had been working as intelligently as he knew how, with the Commission Council's full and complete cooperation, to cope with the racial unrest. "I have reason to believe that our situation is in good condition at this time."

No mention in Cutrer's reply about appointing the committee suggested by Talley, but two years later the city had its all-white Community Affairs Committee and the Blacks and the Voters League had their all-black Bi-Racial Committee.

There were some very good men on the city's new committee, though, and I'm sure the mayor did what he thought was the right thing when he named an all-white group. They met in Cutrer's office at City Hall on March 29 and called for "composure" by all Bogalusans. The group was to become very active in the days ahead.

In April, the paper received a letter, which had probably been sent to newspapers across the South—maybe even the country—from Alabama's Governor George Wallace. It was an invitation for the editor to come to Alabama to join a four-day media tour of the state, which was having racial troubles of its own.

"Has the news from Alabama been distorted?" the governor opened the letter. "Is Alabama a state where fear stalks its streets? Is Alabama still living in the dark ages? Why doesn't your editor determine for himself the true Alabama story?"

I don't know how many journalists took the governor up on his invitation, but I wasn't one of them.

A few days later, a day of "restaurant testing" was held in Jonesboro, Louisiana. Blacks were served at three restaurants that day and turned away at three others.

Five days later on April 8, big trouble spilled out into the streets of Bogalusa. The main street downtown was blocked to traffic. Students from the all-black Central Memorial High School began a march from the school to Columbia Street a half-block away. They were stopped by city police, who refused to let them march from East Seventh Street onto Columbia Street because they did not have a permit.

The night before, someone had left a coffin in front of the Black Union Hall. The sign they placed on the coffin bore the word "CORE" and illuminated it with flares and spotlights.

Earlier on the day of the blocked student march, shots had reportedly been fired at the home of Robert Hicks, where the CORE worker from Boston, William Yates, was staying. Hicks said bricks were thrown at the window of his Volkswagen parked in front of his house. He came out of the house and fired two shots at the car from which the bricks were thrown as it sped away. Witnesses said several shots were fired back from the getaway car, but nobody was hit.

Bogalusa stores found Black pickets put up in front of their buildings at 1:30 the next afternoon, and it was announced that CORE Director Farmer was due in town that day to lead a night rally at Central Memorial High.

Farmer spoke to the rally that night and told the crowd that Mayor Cutrer had refused to meet with him to discuss Blacks' demands. Farmer also said that he had originally planned to leave the city the next day, but because of the mounting tensions he was going to stay in Bogalusa indefinitely. That decision only led to added tensions in the city, with the Klan still determined to block racial integration.

Shortly thereafter, the Bogalusa Civic and Voters League sent a letter to the mayor listing the following demands:

1. Equal economic opportunity in public and private employment and in city licensing practices.
2. Equal educational opportunities in integrated school facilities.
3. Desegregation of all public accommodations and facilities.
4. Extension to all of the community of sewerage, paved roads, bright street lighting and adequate enforced housing codes.
5. Inclusion of Negro leaders on a decision-making level in the city and parish and on industrial development planning boards.

6. Removal from city ordinances of all unconstitutional discriminatory laws.
7. Employment of Negro city policemen with all proper police power to help issue the equal enforcement of law.

Mayor Cutrer responded with a letter stating that the Commission Council would meet with representatives of the Voters League to discuss the demands, but the letter did not include a suggested timeline for such a meeting.

The next day, Friday, April 9, things got out of hand. Shortly after 9:00 a.m. Black marchers, who had gathered downtown at the corner of Columbia and East Third Streets, were just getting started on their city-approved march down Columbia Street. Some 200 white bystanders angrily waded into the Black crowd, swinging at them with fists and signs they were carrying. Police hurriedly moved into the fracas. A police car struck one of the whites who was in the middle of the street with the angry mob. A state policeman screamed, "Get the hell out of the way and let this car through."

There was mass confusion and yelling by both sides as police finally brought order from chaos. A news photographer from New Orleans and an FBI agent were both struck by whites during the melee. Police ordered the marchers to turn back to prevent further violence and gradually the shouting and shoving eased.

Within an hour, however, many of the whites who had just angrily left downtown began gathering in front of City Hall, which was to have been the destination for the Black marchers who started on Columbia Street. Between 200 and 300 whites milled around outside City Hall, waiting. But they waited in vain as the march by the Blacks had been aborted.

The parking lot of the Pine Tree Plaza Shopping Center near City Hall was filled with cars and pickup trucks—many bearing Confederate Flag plates on their front bumpers—of the whites who had gathered in front of City Hall. The crowd began dispersing about 10:30 a.m., and within a half-hour they were all gone.

Mayor Cutrer, who had reportedly refused on Thursday to meet with Farmer, did meet with him following the Friday morning street battle. Farmer said the Blacks planned to march again that afternoon and demanded protection. Cutrer assured him that there would be no violence in the second attempt to march.

It was not generally known that these assurances had been made, or how they could be kept in light of the morning battle. But that afternoon about 400 Blacks and 11 whites marched peacefully under heavy police escort from downtown along Columbia Street and to City Hall. The mayor had kept his word; his policemen had listened.

The weekend, surprisingly, passed quietly—at least on the surface. A quiet tension prevailed day and night as the townspeople waited for the next battle. On Monday morning, April 12, CORE announced that it was postponing its picketing at local businesses pending talks between Black leaders, Cutrer, the Commission Council, and local merchants.

But the truce fell apart almost immediately. There was brief picketing downtown by Black leaders again on Wednesday the 14th. The pickets left at noon as local businessmen told the Blacks that they should broaden their base, that there were three Black groups in the city and that the Voters League did not represent the entire Black community.

Pickets were up again on Thursday, April 15, as Blacks continued to press for "job equality." Whites counter-picketed with anti-black slogans on their signs alleging links by CORE to communism and to the National Council of Churches, which they apparently thought was a bad thing. Black picketing and white counter-picketing continued without incident on Friday and the following Monday—picketers on both sides took the weekend off—and there was a quiet march by Blacks in the rain on Monday, April 19.

By Tuesday, April 20, there was a noticeable buildup in the number of police showing up downtown. James Farmer, who had left town briefly, was back that day and led another march to City Hall, where he called for answers to the seven-point list of demands that had been submitted to the mayor by the Voter's League the previous week.

8

CORE, GO HOME

1965

Neither whites nor Blacks were giving an inch. There was a virtual stalemate as the picketing continued and the counter-picketing followed suit. Farmer's presence was making white opinion crystallize against the Black cause. Addressing that point, I wrote an editorial challenging CORE's tactics. It ran on page one on the afternoon of Thursday, April 22:

FROM RIDICULOUS TO MORE RIDICULOUS

The latest episode of CORE picketing in front of City Hall demonstrates by itself the regress from the ridiculous to the more ridiculous.

In front of Bogalusa's City Hall yesterday were children holding signs about freedom, jobs and removal of Mayor Jesse H. Cutrer Jr. from office. CORE appears to be lashing out in desperation here, for its leader, James Farmer, obviously has not been able to get the kind of support he wants. True, he has gotten more than his share of publicity, but the story is beginning to be "old hat."

Seasoned newsmen from much of the South have seen this pattern of CORE in one place after another. CORE figures if it yells loud enough and long enough, it will get backing . . .

The city administration set up the machinery for a survey to determine the Negro leadership in Bogalusa. Six men have been working on the survey for a week in order that city officials would know who the Negro leadership is.

As soon as this became known to Farmer and CORE, they rallied a few hundred high school students and had them going from door to door signing up people for the CORE cause. And before any announcement of the results of the city survey could be made, CORE announced that 98 percent of the voting age Negroes in the city support the Bogalusa Civic and Voters League. This is CORE's claim, which is obviously a grossly exaggerated claim. But that is the same old trick. The city was having a responsible survey made to come up with a sound answer, but before anything could be compiled, CORE makes its grand announcement that 98 percent back CORE and the Voters League.

This leads to more dissension—exactly what CORE wants . . .

It has all gone from the ridiculous to the more ridiculous with CORE. It is our fervent hope that somebody will get through to Farmer and his gang that this city should no more be his target than any other city in this country.

He is not wanted here, CORE is not wanted here. Farmer is looking out for Farmer and the people of Bogalusa know it.

It was pretty harsh criticism, and the city's and parish's Black community probably felt that CORE had their best interests at heart. But I thought at the time that CORE, or at least Farmer, had their own interests in mind.

Farmer made another speech that night, at the Greater Ebenezer Baptist Church. About 500 Blacks attended, many of them students who had participated in the marches. State Public Service Director Tom Burbank also ordered 300 more state troopers into Bogalusa as peacekeepers, obviously on orders from the Governor John McKeithen in the state capitol.

From out of the blue came an offer for mediation. Three Louisiana notables offered their services to mediate the race problem between Bogalusa's Blacks and whites. The three were Louisiana AFL-CIO President Victor Bussie, the powerful labor leader who had been heckled by whites when he spoke to the Rotary Club; Alexandria attorney Camille

Gravel, an upper echelon politico in the state; and New Orleans State Senator Michael O'Keefe.

Mayor Cutrer said he would accept their suggestions, turn them over to the Commission Council, and seek the advice of the Bogalusa Community Affairs Committee. A. Z. Young, the new president of the Black Voters League and gaining in leadership stature and presence in the Black community as one of the founders of the Deacons for Defense, said he would accept the offer of mediation.

This all sounded good. The mayor was willing to listen to outside mediators and the most vocal of the Black leadership said the same thing. Was this the light at the end of the tunnel that Bogalusa moderates had hoped for?

Bogalusa, however, was not that fortunate. A Black minister in town stated publicly that he was against demonstrations and marches and spoke out against CORE and others who had branded him and other moderate Blacks as "Uncle Toms."

On April 15, an editorial questioned the timing of the new Black picketing of stores in the city's main business district.

A TIME FOR GOOD FAITH

After threats for weeks, pickets finally appeared in front of our stores in Bogalusa yesterday on Columbia Street. They were back again today.

It was surprising to see the pickets demonstrating in front of our places of business, because the machinery was already well in motion to have a merchants group discuss the problems over which the pickets were demonstrating.

It was unfortunate that the pickets should have shown up at the very time that the talks were to have begun. Very few people respond favorably while being shoved around and pressured.

There are apparently many people in the country who feel that the demonstration, the march in the streets, is the thing to use. We disagree. Just as we felt that the Congress of Racial Equality should not have come into our city last week with its pressure tactics, so also do we feel that the pickets in front of the local stores were uncalled for.

If the CORE-inspired people here are serious about wanting to talk with our local businessmen, they should recognize the fact that discussion could be held much more harmoniously without pickets walking the street outside those businessmen's stores . . .

Those who are demonstrating in our streets should take a look at what they are doing. They expect our business people to talk with them at the conference table, but at the same time they try to discredit them, in the streets with their signs and their very presence.

Act in good faith. If you want to talk, don't walk.

Behind the scenes, the movement to establish a hard-core segregation newspaper in Bogalusa was steamrolling. The newsprint salesman was still doing the legwork for the Bogalusa segregationists. I obtained a copy of a letter from the Sales Department of Multi-Ad Services, Inc. that referred to a request for information about Multi's advertising art clipping service for the *Times Enterprise*. But a newspaper called the *Times-Enterprise* never appeared on the streets of Bogalusa.

One Sunday morning about that time, my mother in Jefferson Parish had Peg and me listed in the prayer list of the bulletin for the Easter morning service at Jefferson Presbyterian Church where we had grown up: "Mrs. A. J. Major's son, Lewis, and wife, Peggy Ripp, have been hurt in Bogalousa, La. for their stand in better community relations between white and colored." No matter that my name—and the city's—were misspelled; the prayers were appreciated.

On April 20, our editorial call against CORE was more direct.

CORE, GO HOME

It should be evident to all of us now that the Congress of Racial Equality breeds on strife and turmoil.

During the past several weeks CORE representatives have been in our city and have brought in students from various places to stir things up in Bogalusa. Editorially last week this newspaper suggested that CORE people leave Bogalusa and go back to their own home towns and try to settle their own problems there . . .

National press reports stated yesterday that CORE director James Farmer was heading back to Bogalusa today for an indefinite stay. There is nothing that Farmer can do here but cause trouble. It is very easy to manufacture trouble if you go looking for it. And all of these pickets on our streets and in front of our public buildings can't do anything but harm . . .

So we ask again that CORE leave our city, and that the students who have come here go back where they came from and leave our city and our people alone.

And again the next day, on April 21.

THE SAME OLD PATTERN

CORE is following the same old pattern here as everywhere—making mountains out of molehills.

Their leader, James Farmer, said yesterday Bogalusa was CORE's No. 1 target now in the United States. We wonder: Target for what? For strife, turmoil, dissension?

Two days ago in our city, several hundred Negro children and a few outside white people marched through the main business section to City Hall and made some written demands about police protection and equal law enforcement. Then, yesterday, they marched back the same route with Farmer in the lead to get their answer at City Hall.

Mayor J. H. Cutrer Jr. told them before the march he would deliver the answer personally to them and that the march would not be necessary. But they marched anyhow, because that's all part of the plan. Getting an answer without a march would have been too simple . . .

But Farmer is getting just what he always looks for—the television cameras grinding out the film of his news conferences, marches and pickets. If the cameras want some pictures of pickets, they should be in New Orleans right down on Canal Street and find them regularly. They've been there for months.

CORE is not needed here and CORE is not wanted here and the sooner Farmer and his cohorts leave Bogalusa and go prey on somebody else, the sooner we will have normalcy in our city.

The April 25 editorial noted the heavy outside police presence that had come into the city along with CORE, and a judgment that the city administration was winning in its effort to keep things calm in the city.

THE POLICE IN OUR CITY

During the past several weeks, law enforcement officers have been very much in evidence in our city. In addition to City of Bogalusa Police, there have been Police Auxiliary Bogalusa firemen deputized for work, the Washington Parish Sheriff's Department and the Louisiana State Police.

At first, it was a shock to see the streams of State Police cars moving into the city. One morning a caravan of 19 cars drove down the middle of Columbia Street. It looked like the entire State Police force for a while. But later movements of State Police made the 19 cars look like very few.

Men have been working around the clock, standing by their radios and telephones, toiling at preserving law and order.

Unfounded charges of "police brutality" and "unequal enforcement" of the law by CORE have been totally and completely unfair to men who have left their families and homes and spent long, hard hours at work here. The work of all of the men—city, parish, and state—has been exemplary . . .

Bogalusa's administration and its people are winning this war of nerves declared by CORE. Surely, CORE must be feeling the pangs of frustration, because our people have risen above them and refuse to let the outside inflammatory influences of CORE hurt us.

There can be no doubt about it—Bogalusa is winning the struggle and it is now clearer than ever that there is no place in Bogalusa for the Congress of Racial Equality and its leader James Farmer.

That series of editorials criticizing CORE wouldn't have been enough to get me onto the Klan's "good guy" list—that surely wasn't my goal, anyway—and they likely did get me onto the Blacks' "bad guy" list. But, at the time, I thought they were fair because I thought that CORE's tactics were not helpful in trying to maintain a calm atmosphere in the city.

. . . .

In mid-April, Peg and I joined friends of the beleaguered Reverend Shepherd to plan a recognition dinner for him. A vicious Midnight Mail thrown around the city had referred to him as a heavy drinker who was often seen buying liquor at local liquor stores. It also made scurrilous insinuations about Reverend Shepherd because he had living with him a teenaged boy whom he housed as a homeless runaway.

Reverend Shepherd was having quite a bit of trouble within the church, with some parishioners holding back on paying their earlier monetary pledges. One member, whose husband owned an important business in town and who was one of the important contributors to the church, had very recently labeled Reverend Shepherd as a "liar" and refused to attend the dinner.

Late in the month, the former paper mill manager Vertrees Young copied the newspaper on a letter he had sent to Mayor Cutrer: "I spent Wednesday and Thursday attending meetings of PAR (the Louisiana Public Affairs Research Council) and CABL (the Council for a Better Louisiana), along with many other business and professional people from all corners of the state, and it would have gratified you greatly to hear the expressions of praise for your conduct and your handling of this very difficult situation, which I heard on all sides."

On Tuesday night, April 27, three burning crosses were planted on the Episcopal church grounds, where the dinner for Rev. Shepherd was to be held two nights later on Thursday. The crosses at the church immediately brought back memories of Ku Klux Klan threats in January that had resulted in cancellation of Congressman Hays's planned talk about moderation that had been scheduled in the same building. We decided to proceed as planned with the dinner for Reverend Shepherd despite the crosses and the threat they implied.

Eighty-two people attended the testimonial, including the Episcopal Bishop of Louisiana Girault M. Jones and his wife from New Orleans, and the Reverend Father Hubert Bordenave, resident priest at the Annunciation Catholic Church in Bogalusa. Father Bordenave made a moving speech about Reverend Shepherd, characterizing him as a man of high principles who stood strongly by his beliefs.

The day before the testimonial, an organization calling itself the United Conservatives of Washington Parish tried to book the Bogalusa High School football stadium for a rally planned about a week later on May 7. But they were denied use of the stadium by the Bogalusa School Board, which had a standing policy of not allowing use of city school facilities by political or racial groups.

The group's promotion chairman said that it was not a political or racial organization and pressed for use of the stadium. Another spokesman said 10,000 were expected for the mass white rally. Members of the group said the gathering was not to be a political or racial event, and continued to press for use of the stadium—which would not have held 10,000 people.

Refused the use of the BHS stadium, the United Conservatives then sought permission to stage the rally in the Pine Tree Plaza Shopping Center parking lot near City Hall, but they were denied by the owner of the property. Finally, the group said it would hold the rally in the city-owned Goodyear Park, next to the "white" YMCA on Avenue B and a stone's throw from the high school football stadium. Since the earliest days of the city, the park had been the site of political rallies and major gatherings of all sorts.

Amidst all of this white activity, the three out-of-town mediators and attorneys met to try to set up negotiations between Bogalusa Blacks and whites.

On May 1, a new face came onto the Bogalusa scene. Black comedian and activist Dick Gregory came to the city and spoke on Black rights in a vacant lot in a Black area of town. Most people in the city saw this as a negative in the cause of mediation between the races.

A few nights later, on Wednesday, May 5, Mayor Cutrer was back on the local radio. He told the people of Bogalusa that while the United Conservatives of Washington Parish had asked for a parade permit for Friday night, May 7, he and the Commission Council did not feel it was the right time or place for such a parade or march. He also said the United Conservatives had not asked to use Goodyear Park for the rally. So while everybody was thinking the rally would be held in the park, the mayor denied that the United Conservatives had even asked for permission to use it.

Archconservative Judge Leander Perez, the political boss who was president of the Parish Council in Plaquemines Parish south of New Orleans, had been announced as one of the main speakers for the rally. However, he announced that he did not plan to be a speaker at the rally, and he agreed with Mayor Cutrer and with Louisiana Governor McKeithen that it was the wrong time and place for such a rally to be held. Another scheduled speaker from Alabama also pulled out in deference to the mayor and the governor.

The conservatives then said they would march to the "Goodyear Park area" on Avenue B. That night, the march did take place, with between 2,500 and 3,000 whites taking part. It was by far the largest public demonstration in the city—Black or white—since the period of racial unrest had begun. They paraded to and in front of the YMCA, whose grounds bordered and opened onto Goodyear Park. Actually, it was the all-white YMCA on Avenue B; the YMCA in town also had an all-black facility on the other side of the city, near the newspaper office.

Congressional candidate John Rarick was among the speakers for that rally, as were local Klansmen and noted conservatives from across the state.

Since they had been denied use of Goodyear Park, the crowd gathered at and around a corner service station across the street from the YMCA and in the adjacent Goodyear Park. Rebel flags covered the city all that Friday afternoon. Many out-of-towners congregated near the downtown area while waiting for the start of the rally.

On the day of the gathering of conservatives, a Bogalusa policeman, in uniform, called the *Daily News* a "Communist newspaper" in front of a group of people gathered in front of the Acme Cafe on Columbia Street. I wrote a letter of protest to Commissioner of Safety Arnold Spiers, with copies to the mayor and Police Chief Claxton Knight.

The following Saturday morning, Police Captain Haynes "Twister" Wascom and a patrolman from the police department came to the newspaper office and talked to the boy who had heard the policeman's statement to which I had protested. The youth went to police headquarters with the officers and identified the policeman. The patrolman who had escorted the young carrier to the police station came back to see me and said that Safety Commissioner Arnold Spiers, Police Chief Claxton Knight, and Assistant Police Chief L. C. Terrell were going to talk to the new policeman. The patrolman was very apologetic on behalf of his superiors.

The night before, on the night of the whites' rally, someone put a KKK sticker on the windshield of my car in our driveway, and let the air out of the tires of the car. They even went so far as to also let the air out of the tires of the bicycle, parked under our carport, that Lou Jr. used to run his afternoon paper route. It was pretty tame stuff, but it was unsettling to know that people of hostile intent had been under our carport in the night.

A break in the stalemate came on Saturday, May 15, when Mayor Cutrer said that city officials would talk with the Bogalusa Voters

League. In another radio address announcing the meetings, the mayor said a statement of principles should be made public: ". . . Tonight, I want to discuss with you some of these laws and principles."

He cited laws guaranteeing the rights—all without discrimination based on race, color, or creed—of all people to have equal protection under the law, to vote, to use of public facilities and have equal accommodations and services, to equal employment opportunities, and to equal educational opportunities.

He stated that while the City of Bogalusa could not be the official enforcer of many of these laws, it also could not block their enforcement by other appropriate government agencies.

I have on many occasions told you that the Mayor, Commission Council and City Attorney stand for law and order, and we will, during the coming times in Bogalusa, stand by that pledge.

In that connection, we can provide for the people who are exercising their rights and the people who are subject to these laws, full and impartial police protection. We, as your elected officials, pledge that our fine police department . . . will give full protection to everyone and will give it impartially.

Bogalusa has always been a peaceful town. The eyes of the rest of the South and the entire nation are upon us now. Had we been given the choice, I know we would have chosen to mind our own business. But suddenly our business is the business of the South and the nation . . . We can only start with what principles we have and work hard and sincerely to do what is right. It is for these reasons that we, the Mayor, Commission Council and City Attorney have chosen to go to the meeting table and to state these principles.

On Sunday, the next day, city officials and Voters League representatives met, with the three outside mediators—Bussie, Gravel, and O'Keefe—sitting in as "observers." No official proclamations came out of the meeting, but Voters League secretary Gayle Jenkins labeled the session as "totally unsatisfactory."

In the aftermath of the meeting, the scene for violence shifted to Bogalusa's Cassidy Park, on the eastern bank of Bogue Lusa Creek. On Wednesday, May 19, CORE and the Voters League attempted to integrate the park. In those times, Blacks were not allowed to go into Cassidy Park; it was one of many places that were off limits to them.

And when forty to fifty Blacks moved into the park that afternoon, a group of young whites attacked them. Afterward, charges and counter-charges were made as to who hit whom and who mistreated whom and that police used dogs on the Blacks.

The next day, the city shut the park down completely when several hundred whites gathered there waiting for the Blacks to return. White teens grabbed the camera of a New Orleans newspaper photographer. The photographer chased them and others chased him, and when the gang of whites caught the photographer they beat him and smashed the camera. The photographer and his broken camera got a police escort out of town.

9

A BOLT OUT OF THE BLUE

1965

On Sunday night, May 23, Mayor Cutrer was back on the radio yet again, this time to announce that all public facilities in the City of Bogalusa would henceforth be desegregated, that Black policemen would be hired by the city police department, that jobs in other departments of the city administration would be opened up to Blacks, and that unconstitutional city segregation laws in Bogalusa would be repealed.

It was a momentous announcement. It was like a bolt out of the blue. The Black community had made a gigantic jump forward in this small Southern paper mill town.

The KKK and Klan-types became embittered at Cutrer immediately. At City Hall that night there also appeared a sign which read "Nigger Town, USA," an obvious reaction to Mayor Cutrer's new position of compromise. So while the city was being labeled "Klantown USA" by outside journalists, the KKK was taking the opposite view with a label of its own.

The next day, whites tried to take control of the still-closed Cassidy Park by tearing down the gates that had been erected by the city to keep out vehicles—whether driven by Blacks or whites. City police kept them out.

Two days after Cutrer's radio address, the *Chicago Sun Times* wrote an editorial—"Racial Tension Is Costly"—reminding that the new Civil Rights Act included the authority for the federal government to cut off federal funding to any program or activity in which discrimination is practiced. The editorial noted Cutrer's new conciliatory stance, observing, "Communities that still do discriminate are beginning to get the message. Discrimination always has been costly, but this was not always apparent. The experience of Bogalusa and the threat of a cut-off of federal funds sounds the message loud and clear. Bogalusa, for one, not only should be a better town but a more prosperous one when it repeals desegregation ordinances."

That same day, on Tuesday, May 25, Community Affairs Council Chairman John Gallaspy announced that the work of the three mediators— Bussie, Gravel, and O'Keefe—was concluded. "The worst is over," he said.

Little did he know.

The next night was Class Night at Central Memorial High School and whites and Blacks massed out on the street near the school, the different-colored crowds only a block apart. All the ingredients for a bloody battle were in place. For a long time both Blacks and whites lingered quietly, anticipating an all-out street battle. Fortunately, the quiet calm prevailed. Nothing happened, and in about an hour the crowd dispersed.

On Thursday, May 27, Voters League President A. Z. Young said that the local Blacks' "truce" was off, because white merchants in town refused to discuss making jobs available for them in their stores. As he declared that Black picketing of businesses would resume, the stage had once again been set for violence.

The (white) Bogalusa Citizens Council began circulating petitions for the recall of Mayor Cutrer, citing the mayor's giving in to civil rights pressures as grounds. But the petition never made it through the legal process and a recall election against Cutrer was never held. A year later he would decline to run for reelection.

On Sunday, May 30, Bogalusa's industrial elder statesman Vertrees Young, who had for many years carried considerable weight and influence in and for Bogalusa by virtue of his long tenure as the top boss at the local paper mill, called for an end to boycotts and threats in Bogalusa. But his voice, even as president of the statewide Council for a Better Louisiana, was now little more than a voice in the wilderness.

Everything that was taking place in Bogalusa was getting its share of national publicity. On May 5, 1965, nationally syndicated columnists

Rowland Evans and Robert Novak, in their *Inside Report* column titled "CORE vs. the Klan," drew this picture of the city and its problems on May 5, 1965: "It was Bogalusa's experience to have radicals on both sides of the racial conflict—the violent, shameful, white-supremacist Ku Klux Klan for the whites, and the non-violent idealistic, but militant Congress of Racial Equality (CORE) for the Negroes."

Evans and Novak laid the blame for the state of affairs at the feet of "pious and platitudinous" Mayor Cutrer.

They wrote that the Klan had paraded in full KKK regalia on Columbia Street with a permit issued by Cutrer.

"With such semi-official sanction" Evans and Novak wrote, "the Klan got bolder. Crosses were burned, hate literature was distributed castigating Bogalusa's white moderates, and bricks were tossed through windows." They continued their criticism of Cutrer, noting the city's refusal to allow use of City Hall for the meeting with Representative Brooks Hays.

But Evans and Novak then took a turn and credited "a new Jesse Cutrer" for a late change of heart that helped avert open racial confrontation: "For the first time the mayor preached law and order and worked for racial amity."

They concluded by conceding that, at the time of their writing, "Bogalusa is no haven of love" and "[t]he hope of Bogalusa lies in the possibility that the submerged moderates will come to the fore while the extremists on both sides fade away."

Meanwhile, the Klan was working on the "big picture" with its threats and intimidations aimed at individuals. The *Daily News* received a handwritten letter on May 14 from a man in Varnado, in northeast Washington Parish: "I have received a threatening letter concerning my welfare of me and my family. I work and provide for my family, and anytime anybody wants any of what I have got, I keep it with me at all times. . . . If you KKK's will mind your own business we will get along fine."

I assume he was referencing having a gun with him at all times, but it was one of those rare instances in which somebody spoke out publicly against the Klan.

To bolster its contention that Blacks in Bogalusa did not have equal job opportunities, the Bogalusa Voters League conducted a survey of 1964 economic status of area Blacks. The study took note of "the annual earnings of 1,303 Negro citizens representing 20 industries, businesses, professions and employees" in special categories.

According to the study, the aggregate annual income of the group studied in 1964 was $5,567,300. The largest group of Blacks in the study was in the paper mill, where 300 were employed with aggregate annual wages of $1,560,000—an average of $5,200 a year. Woodcutters and construction workers represented a total of 310 workers whose combined wages were $1,299,200—averaging $1,000 less per year than the mill workers. Among Blacks employed in organizations owned and operated by Blacks, there were 128 concerns which paid an aggregate in wages and salaries of $365,760. School teachers, maids, laundry workers, domestics, and beauticians were cited as the principal occupations open to Black women and girls.

According to the study, more than 90 percent of all Black males were employed in unskilled, semiskilled, and service occupations. H. H. Guy, a local Black insurance executive who assisted in collecting the data said, "Because of the limited employment opportunities open to Negro youth, we find every year the vast majority of the better trained and educated leave Bogalusa for New Orleans, Houston, Dallas and Northern communities."

William Bailey Jr. of the Voters League said that twenty-one Black churches in Bogalusa had a membership of about 2,100. "The churches represent the most important organized group life activity among Negroes in the city," he said.

Both Bailey and Guy, longtime residents of the city, extolled the many fine relations which existed between Blacks and whites. "White race relations here are not ideal," said Guy, (but) "they are far better here than many cities in the state." Bailey said there were few businesses and industrial concerns in the city that did not benefit from Black patronage. He urged more liberal employment for qualified Blacks and more opportunities for responsible Blacks and whites to sit around the table to discuss problems of race relations. "After all, Negroes and whites in Bogalusa have more common interests than differences."

The *Delta Democrat Times* in Greenville, Mississippi, noted as an enlightened Southern moderate newspaper under the editorship of the famed Hodding Carter, took note of a comparison between Bogalusa and Natchez, Mississippi. Carter was a Louisiana native, Pulitzer Prize–winning journalist who challenged the spread of archconservatism in his own paper. Less than a month after Evans and Novak blistered Mayor Cutrer's handling of the situation, Carter shone some of Cutrer's later actions in a better light. In a May 25 editorial, Carter wrote:

> Bogalusa may finally have turned the corner, despite inevitable trouble still ahead from the organized racists . . .
>
> Mayor Cutrer said he would ask the city to repeal all its existing segregation statutes and to open all its facilities to all people, regardless of race.
>
> Obviously Mayor Cutrer and the community leadership which backed him in his decision are going to catch hell from the Ku Kluxers and their sympathizers. But Bogalusa's troubles will at least be those of a community which is at last facing reality and is seeking to deal with it . . .
>
> We would not want to be Mayor Cutrer of Bogalusa in the next few months, because some of the white reaction to what he has done is bound to be bitter. . . . Bogalusa has apparently faced up to facts, so while it still must pass over a rocky road it has at least set out on the journey.

And a grueling journey it was that still lay ahead.

Things had been relatively quiet for more than a week, but another fuse had been burning all the while. On Monday, May 31, another wild street battle ensued between Blacks and whites in downtown Bogalusa. Black pickets in front of Columbia Street stores were attacked by whites.

Concealed weapons were found, a snake was let loose, and fireworks exploded, so police waded into the melee to try to restore order. Finally, after twenty-eight arrests, the fighting stopped.

Mayor Cutrer responded angrily by charging that Blacks had "broken faith." He decreed that no more marches or demonstrations would be allowed in Bogalusa until tension eased, and the city issued new orders pertaining to march routes, hours, and numbers of people allowed. Both sides reacted angrily, loudly claiming their right to peaceful assembly. But "peaceful" was the missing element of the May 31 outbreak that had sparked the changes by the city.

White attackers who waged the street battle that day used a new diversionary tactic for the first time. While most of them remained on Columbia Street near the Black pickets, a smaller group went a block away and staged a sham fight. That attracted most of the police from Columbia Street, and when the police were lured to that fake fracas, the whites on Columbia Street waded into the Black pickets.

There were no arrests following the fights, but police warned both sides to disperse and not to return. As usual, the warnings fell on deaf ears. The next day, twenty Black picketers were back in front of Columbia Street businesses. But this time there was no violence.

Mayor Cutrer publicly stated his disagreement with the May 25 statement by Community Affairs Council Chairman Gallaspy that the work of the three out-of-town mediators Bussie, Gravel, and O'Keefe was over. But Cutrer did add that black-white negotiations in the city were "at a standstill." Surprisingly, the state police who had been assigned to Bogalusa for weeks left town that same day, leaving the city under the protection of the understaffed Bogalusa Police Department.

It was on the very next night, Wednesday, June 2, 1965, that one of the most heinous crimes of racial violence in Washington Parish—or anywhere—occurred.

A year and a day after they were hired as the first Black sheriff's deputies in Washington Parish, Oneal Moore and Creed Rogers were victims of a deadly ambush while patrolling the streets in the Village of Varnado, seven miles northeast of Bogalusa in northeastern Washington Parish. At 10:00 p.m., a hail of bullets from a passing pickup truck tore into both deputies while Deputy Moore was driving himself and Deputy Rogers to Moore's nearby home for them to get something to eat. The patrol car went out of control and crashed into a tree. Deputy Moore was rushed to a Bogalusa hospital but was pronounced dead on arrival. He was thirty-four years old. Deputy Rogers was seriously wounded and lost his right eye, but he recovered and returned to duty as deputy.

Shortly after eleven o'clock that night, Bogalusan Ernest Ray McElveen, forty-one, was arrested in his pickup truck in Tylertown, Mississippi, and was charged with murder. He was alone at the time, although police investigations proved that at least two men, and possibly three, were involved in the nightrider attack.

The community and parish were in a state of shock. Street marches, fistfights, picketing, name-calling, boycotting and the like were one thing, but a night-rider murder was quite another. The shame of it all, however, is that no one other than McElveen was ever arrested, and the McElveen case was never brought before a Grand Jury due to lack of evidence. The murder weapons were never found. McElveen was released on $25,000 bond nine days after he was jailed.

When the foreman of the Washington Parish Grand Jury tried to have the case called before the body, District Attorney Woodrow "Squinch" Erwin would not bring it in. He said there was not sufficient evidence to prosecute, and he couldn't get a conviction if the Grand Jury did indict McElveen. The D.A. was said to have been fearful that the Grand Jury wanted to rush the case before its members, indict McElveen, and have him go to trial and be found innocent.

There were no murder weapons and there were no eyewitnesses. It would have been a very weak case and Erwin knew it. Time passed and McElveen was effectively cleared when the charges were dropped.

Whatever was the truth about that awful event, it never came out.

Moore's name is among those engraved on the memorial to victims of racial violence in the plaza at the Civil Rights Memorial Center in Montgomery, Alabama.

Twenty-four years later, in December 1989, the FBI announced that it had received new information in the case and was reopening its investigation into the ambush killing of Deputy Moore. During the last week of January 1990, agents accompanied the Bogalusa unit of the Louisiana National Guard to a house north of Bogalusa. The local National Guard was an engineering unit, and Guardsmen used their heavy equipment to dig up a concrete slab next to the house.

They were reportedly searching for the murder weapons used in Deputy Moore's 1965 slaying, but after several days of digging, the agency said it had found nothing, and called off the digging. Even though the agency said it had received new information in the meantime and would continue the investigation, the case was closed—unsolved—in 2016.

After he recovered, Creed Rogers went back to work at the Sheriff's Office, and he retired as a captain on the force in 1988. He died in 2007 at the age of eighty-four.

Two days after Deputy Moore was killed on that early June night in 1965, a white deputy sheriff reported that shots were fired at his rural house south of Bogalusa during the night. The shooting fit no pattern and it was never determined how that incident fit into the ongoing racial problems of the area. Some speculated that the shots at a white deputy's home were in protest of the killing of the Black deputy Moore two nights earlier.

With summer facing the city, racial tension and violence still a major part of our lives, and young people leaving the school rooms, it was feared that some terrible days were upon us. On Wednesday, June 9, I ran the following page one editorial calling for—and hoping for—a summer of peace and not hostility.

OUR SUMMER OF YEARNING

Bogalusa is on the threshold of summer. The kids are all out of school for their favorite time of the year—vacation. School books are put away for three months, the late-sleepers get a chance to be a little lazy, while the early-uppers still bounce out of their beds at the crack of dawn, taking advantage of every daylight hour to go about the urgent business of play and good times.

. . . Our Summer this year is much like that of all our previous Summers, except . . .

Except that our people are troubled. There is a distinct feeling of uneasiness. Our days begin with uncertainty . . .

Our people are unfortunately restless, wary, suspecting. We must find normalcy to our lives, we must again recognize the joy and beauty of doing a day's work, enjoying the companionship of friends and leisurely weekends. Somehow, some way, we must rid ourselves of the fears which have beset us.

We have lost the way to life. We have lost much of the joy of being free, God-fearing citizens of the United States of America.

Too many of our people have become obsessed with one "cause" or another, at the same time forgetting the simple beauties of a Sunday afternoon drive through our beautiful countryside, a walk through the park, a child splashing playfully in a pool, a mockingbird singing his night song, a field of black-eyed Susans waving in the wind.

We must find the way as individuals, for only then can our city and our community-wide area become a haven for peaceful people who wish to enjoy their earthly existence.

The answer lies within each of us. The government cannot solve our problem. No organization, no leader, no cause can show us the way back to the tranquility of a good life. It lies only within ourselves . . .

Let us—each of us—find anew the appreciation of so wonderful a life as we have within our grasp. Nobody has to give it to us, nobody has to show us how—it is ours only through peace and understanding.

An exchange of letters at this same time was more evidence of the strain on everybody in the city. Charles J. Cassidy, a former mayor of Bogalusa and Chairman of the Board of First State Bank and Trust Company, sent a letter to Mayor Cutrer on June 7. Cassidy was fairly well regarded as the most financially powerful man in Bogalusa. Then the President of the Louisiana Bankers Association, Cassidy told Cutrer that state and regional banks that held City of Bogalusa municipal bonds had expressed concern over Bogalusa's municipal credit rating "in light of the adverse publicity received . . .

"So that I can pass on to those who have already asked for it any constructive information with respect to our city's finances," he added, "I will greatly appreciate it if you will make available to me a copy of the most recent audit together with any data you would like to contribute."

A few days later, Cutrer responded on June 11: "I hope the audit of the City Government for the year 1964 has given you some help with the members of the Louisiana Bankers Association," he wrote. "As President of this organization, I am sure your opinion will carry much weight. . . . I remind you that Bogalusa was first spotlighted by some local citizens who stirred the Klan issue in the Brooks Hays matter. This was the beginning of all our trouble and this, in my opinion, is the reason Bogalusa was selected as the number one target for the unholy and unchristian CORE organization."

It is worth noting that in responding to Cassidy, the mayor had laid all of the city's Ku Klux Klan activity at the feet of the Committee of Six that invited Brooks Hays to speak in the city. Cutrer wrote to Cassidy that it was that invitation that had "stirred the Klan," and that had been the "the beginning of all our trouble" in December 1964 and January 1965.

Cutrer had apparently forgotten a full year of "stirred Klan" activity in 1964: cross-burnings across the Florida Parishes (including Bogalusa) in January, a public threat against me at a Klan rally in April, the testing by Blacks of the downtown lunch counters in the face of mobs of angry whites in July, activity by CORE and the Bi-Racial Committee in the summer, more crosses in August, and several issues of the Midnight Mail throughout the year.

If the mayor felt that all of Bogalusa's troubles had started in December 1965, why had he attempted in July 1964 to coordinate the local news blackout of "racial" news with the *Daily News* and the city's two radio stations?

On Saturday, June 12, about 100 Black Bogalusa young people were taken to the state capitol in Baton Rouge, where they demonstrated on the front steps calling for police protection of Black pickets in Bogalusa.

There was a period of comparative quiet for the next two weeks, while Black picketers continued to parade in front of Columbia Street businesses.

But on Tuesday, June 29, there was a fistfight in front of a store on Columbia Street when a Black picket and the store's owner exchanged words.

The city also put the gates back up in front of Cassidy Park to keep everybody out. While the park was officially closed, Blacks claimed it was still being used by whites. It was another unfortunate circumstance for everybody in the city: the only large park in town was shut down during the summer.

The gates that the city had put up at Cassidy Park on June 29 were torn down again during the night on Monday, July 5. It was widely assumed that Blacks had torn down the gates, but some argued steadfastly that white extremists had done it in defiance to the city's attempts to prevent fights between the races.

The Voters League and CORE announced that they would intensify their demonstrations the next week, stating that CORE's national director James Farmer would return to the city, along with two celebrity Black activists: comedian Dick Gregory and singer Harry Belafonte. The Voters League announced that demonstrations would resume after the Independence Day break and would continue until Blacks got better jobs and there was an end to what they called police brutality.

The first thing the city did on that Tuesday, July 6, was to truck in dirt and deposit it in huge mounds on the two roads leading into Cassidy Park—an acknowledgment that it did no good to merely place gates at the park entrances.

On Wednesday, July 7, 350 Black protesters led by Voters League President A. Z. Young walked from downtown to City Hall. Young, at the conclusion of the morning march, said they would march to City Hall again that afternoon.

A crack in their forces occurred that day when CORE Field Secretary Isaac Reynolds told a Black rally: "CORE is wasting its money here."

He said not enough money was being raised among Bogalusa Blacks to carry on the fight.

Meanwhile, from two states away in Birmingham, Alabama, the National States Rights Party announced that rallies for whites would be held in Bogalusa on Thursday, Friday, and Saturday in a field at the corner of Union Avenue and Rio Grande Street near the northwest corner of the city. The Birmingham-based group called for an end to "race-mixing."

On Thursday afternoon, July 8, Blacks marched once more to City Hall, this time under the added protection of 200 Louisiana state troopers who had been sent back into the city by Governor McKeithen. The governor blamed both Blacks and whites in Bogalusa for the ongoing violence and tension, declaring, "We say a plague on both their houses."

In the years since that time, there have been unconfirmed rumors that the governor had sent an emissary to Bogalusa in 1965, with instructions to buy peace in the area by giving $5,000 to the local Klan and an equal amount to the Deacons for Defense. No one knows if this actually occurred, but is interesting to speculate about whether it would have been before or after the governor declared his plague on both houses—those houses being the whites and their Klan, and the Blacks and their Deacons.

More fights broke out downtown on Saturday, July 10, as picketers and white hecklers battled on Columbia Street.

Sunday, July 11, could have been a day marked in blood. CORE and the National States Rights Party both staged marches that afternoon. With a sea of Confederate flags waving, 500 whites marched north on Columbia Street at 2:00 p.m. Only a block away from the starting point of the white march, 500 Blacks were gathering for the 2:30 start of their own march.

The governor had sent in 125 more state troopers during the weekend, the force in the city now totaling 325 uniformed state police. They were braced for the worst and held up the Black marchers until the whites had marched up Columbia Street past the paper mill for several blocks, turned around at the Columbia Street Bridge over the Bogue Lusa Creek, and returned to their starting point.

Only the imagination can explore what might have happened had the two huge crowds of whites and Blacks met on Columbia Street that afternoon. Things were bad enough as it was. At one point as the Blacks marched, some whites set off a string of firecrackers and the Black marchers, fearing it was gunfire, stopped immediately, trying to find out where the "shots" were coming from.

Assistant Chief of Police L. C. Terrell got out of his lead patrol car, bullhorn and machine gun at the ready. "Keep it going!" he yelled out at the Black marchers, fearful that if they stopped for long there would be a serious confrontation. That had become standard procedure for the police: keep things moving, don't let it stop. Protective police had machine guns, sawed-off shotguns, .30-caliber carbines, and gas masks. Two state police helicopters circled overhead.

It was a tense, frightful hot summer afternoon. Only through the grace of God and the welcome presence of a small army of state troopers and local policemen was a bloody battle avoided.

The next day, A. Z. Young and Robert Hicks of the Voters League flew on Governor McKeithen's airplane from Bogalusa to Baton Rouge for talks. The governor asked the Black leaders for a thirty-day moratorium on further demonstrations. That night, when Young and Hicks went before a Black rally back in Bogalusa, Young told them what the governor had asked for.

"No, no!" came cries from the Black crowd. Young told the crowd that he and Hicks had told the governor that they would recommend the cooling-off, but the local Blacks would have no part of it.

That night, whites and Blacks again marched, but there was no fighting this time.

On Tuesday, 375 Blacks marched again, with 325 state troopers guarding them. That night, the Voters League officially turned down Governor McKeithen's request for a thirty-day moratorium, announcing instead that demonstrations would intensify. Two Klan crosses were burned on roadsides near the city that night.

The following day, Wednesday, July 14, as A. Z. Young issued a call for civil rights workers from all over the country to come to Bogalusa and join in the Blacks' battle for "total equality," the state began training 100 agents from the Louisiana Department of Wildlife and Fisheries in riot control. They would soon join the 370 State Police already bivouacked at Bogalusa's National Guard Armory.

A new organization named the "Christian Mothers of Bogalusa" asked for and received a permit and they marched on Columbia Street at 5:30 that afternoon. These were all white women. Blacks also picketed and marched that day, but there were no incidents.

Governor McKeithen flew into Bogalusa for talks with Mayor Cutrer, the Voters League, and the Deacons for Defense. The Ku Klux Klan wasn't invited.

The next day, the scope of Bogalusa's racial battles came into sharper national focus on Thursday, July 15. President Lyndon Johnson ordered John Doar, chief of the US Justice Department's Civil Rights Division, to Bogalusa. This was getting pretty heavy. If the battling whites and Blacks thought they were operating in a vacuum in this little paper mill town, President Johnson's direct involvement must have turned on a light in front of them all.

The picketers had shown up again that day and the Blacks held another rally and marched a block away from Columbia Street on First Avenue. More than 400 Blacks staged their seventh march in eight days, singing spirituals and clapping their hands along the route.

Governor McKeithen ordered police to confiscate any weapons they saw—from whites or Blacks. A. Z. Young objected strenuously, saying that if it weren't for the gun-wielding Black Deacons for Defense, all Bogalusa Blacks would have long before been run out of the city.

John Doar conferred with Governor McKeithen on Thursday night in Baton Rouge and began meeting with city officials the next day. The Blacks marched again downtown on Friday and fights broke out between the marchers and white hecklers. There were sixteen arrests, a mixture of both races.

When the governor pulled 280 of the 370-member state police force from the city, many feared it was an open invitation to the white extremists to resort to violence. Governor McKeithen, in ordering the troopers to leave, said, "There is nothing more I can do." Nobody knew for certain how long the troopers should have stayed in Bogalusa, but it was made clear that the remaining force of ninety was not enough to keep the mobs off the streets.

A. Z. Young, with the situation's fuse obviously shortening, told a Friday night rally: "I do not advocate violence and we are going to do everything we can to keep down the civil war in this area. But if blood is going to be shed, we are going to let it rain down Columbia Street— all kinds, both Black and white. We are not going to send Negro blood down Columbia Street by itself, that's for sure."

It was an open war cry from the most powerful Black voice in the city. Young was regarded as a strong voice of reason, but even he was apparently tiring of the ongoing almost daily street fights. Clearly, he was not backing down from the ongoing battle in the city and surrounding area that had a six-month toll of one murder, two others shot, dozens injured, and more than 100 arrested.

Saturday was another ugly day. After 200 Blacks had marched on Columbia Street to City Hall and then started back toward downtown, they were pelted with rocks, ice, tomatoes, and oranges by onlookers in the Pine Tree Plaza Shopping Center. Black picketers who had shown up in the shopping center parking lot were also drenched with hoses by shop proprietors. A photo of Blacks being hosed by a local barbershop owner made the pages of *Time* magazine.

When the state police, now only ninety-strong, stepped into the fray with raised submachine guns, the pelting and hosing stopped, and the Black marchers were sent on their way.

In the meantime, fully garbed Klansmen in their white robes—but no hoods—were handing out cards and literature downtown announcing a Klan rally scheduled for that night. Hundreds of cars and pickup trucks lined both sides of Mississippi Highway 26 that night as the Klan held its rally, complete with fiery crosses, across the Pearl River in Crossroads, Mississippi.

John Doar had been in Bogalusa less than one week when the long arm of Washington, DC, reached out and put a grip on Bogalusa. The US Justice Department on Monday, July 19, filed in Federal Court in New Orleans seeking an injunction against the Ku Klux Klan. The suit named thirty-five defendants, including twenty Klan members. The injunction request listed the twenty KKK members and fifteen others who were not listed as KKK members but against whom an injunction was also sought.

It was a broad-brush request against the Klan and other defendants, encompassing protection of all the rights of the Black populace without having to fear intimidation, violence, or threats by the Klan and the defendants. The plaintiff was the United States of America, by Attorney General Nicholas Katzenbach, who also filed a request in US District Court for the Eastern District of Louisiana to appoint three judges to hear the injunctive proceedings against the Klan. The heavy artillery had been rolled into place and the Ku Klux Klan and all its cohorts were now under the gun.

On July 29, 1965, Chief Judge Elbert P. Tuttle of the US Fifth Circuit Court, appointed Federal Judges John Minor Wisdom, Herbert W. Christenberry, and Robert A. Ainsworth to hear the Klan case. Everybody in Bogalusa and Washington Parish would get to know those names well.

The sixteen-page federal filing was eye-opening, even to those who lived in the middle of those bleak days. It outlined the many actions that Ku Klux Klan members had taken or planned to hinder Blacks' efforts to exercise their rights to the "free and equal and enjoyment of public facilities, . . . public accommodations, . . . their right to vote and register to vote . . . free from racial discrimination, . . . their right to equal employment opportunities, . . . and their right to equal public educational opportunities on a non-racial basis."

It outlined instances of Klan members and supporters threatening and attacking Blacks as they tried to meet, march, and picket to press their case for equal treatment. It cited incidents or tear gas thrown into Black crowds, plans to burn a Black church, and other anti-Black mayhem.

The filing stated, "Unless restrained by order of this Court, the defendants will continue to engage in conduct similar to that described in this complaint," and "Wherefore, plaintiff (the US Department of Justice) prays that the Court enter a preliminary and permanent injunction enjoining" the Klan and the individual defendants from taking any actions that had been described in the brief.

10
MEETINGS, MARCHES, COURTS, AND CONGRESS
1965

On the same day that the Justice Department filed seeking an injunction against the Klan, July 19, the Blacks marched again in the city, heading for City Hall. This time, however, police stopped them at the south end of the Columbia Street Bridge, telling them to turn back because court was in session in the courtroom at City Hall and the proceedings would not be disturbed or interrupted by demonstrations.

The next afternoon, 230 Blacks held their march back to City Hall. The Klan had been advertising with flyers that there would be another rally the next night, Wednesday, July 20, in an open field at Crossroads, Mississippi, just across the Pearl River from Bogalusa. KKK Imperial Wizard Robert Shelton of Tuscaloosa, Alabama, was to be the main speaker.

Two hundred Blacks marched in the afternoon, and three restaurants served Blacks that day—small numbers compared with the several thousand who showed up that Wednesday night for the Klan rally. It looked like picnic-time as hot dogs, catfish, shrimp, potato chips, pickles, and soft drinks were being sold to the beat of a hillbilly band. Only twenty robed Klansmen were seen among the thousands, their robes emblazoned with letters of United Klans of America, Louisiana province of the Original Ku Klux Klan.

The very familiar Stars and Bars battle flag of the Confederacy waved everywhere. The Stars and Bars had almost become synonymous with the KKK in the Deep South. A gun rack in the back window of a pickup truck and a "Rebel" license plate on the front bumper often meant the driver was KKK, or likely a deep sympathizer for the cause.

On Thursday, July 22, 270 Blacks made another march to City Hall. No whites were on the street; they were virtually empty other than the Black marchers. When they arrived at City Hall at 5:30 p.m., there was nobody there. The absence of white hecklers was puzzling but welcome.

On Saturday, Mayor Cutrer agreed to a request from the Voters League to start holding meetings beginning the following Thursday. Each "side" agreed to be represented by a group of ten. While this bit of negotiating was going on, 252 Blacks marched to City Hall again, without incident. Picketing by Blacks also continued in front of white-owned stores on Columbia Street and in the Pine Tree Plaza Shopping Center near City Hall. Two white pickets showed up in front of the Bogalusa Post Office on Avenue B, picketing the presence of Assistant US Attorney General John Doar.

There were no Black marches on Sunday, Monday, or Tuesday. Black leadership offered no public explanation, but it was thought that the moratorium was a result of Mayor Cutrer's agreement to begin talks with the Voters League the next day, on Thursday.

At the end of the week, on Friday, July 23, Judge Christenberry ordered Bogalusa police to provide protection to Black demonstrators on the street or face fines or imprisonment. At about the same time, another federal judge ordered Bogalusa's two movie theaters—the side-by-side State and Ritz on Columbia Street—to allow Blacks to attend on the same basis as whites by using the front door and no forced balcony seating.

And US District Judge Frank Ellis ordered the Bogalusa City School System desegregated. He ordered grades 1 and 12 desegregated in September of that year; grades 2, 3, 8, 9, and 10 in 1966, and grades 4, 5, 6, 7, and 11 in 1967. With the injunctive suit and the police, movie, and school court orders, the power of the federal government was now being brought to bear on local government and law enforcement.

The next day, Safety Commissioner Arnold Spiers confirmed that two Blacks had passed the city's police qualifying examination. The first two Black policemen in the city's history, Joe White and Louis Brown, would be joining the Bogalusa Police Department in two to three weeks.

The first march in a week was also held that Saturday with 200 Blacks participating. It was held without any trouble, but it was made clear that protestors were not satisfied with the results of the first City–Voters League talks two days before.

Governor McKeithen gave his opinion on the situation in Bogalusa that day. He said he thought that racial trouble in Bogalusa was over. It's strange how politicians often get the notion that saying something is so will make it happen. The worst of the city's racial violence was, perhaps, rapidly cooling down, but there was still trouble ahead. It would soon shift from the streets into the city's schools—but not yet.

Defendants in the USA vs. Klan suit were ordered to appear in Federal Court in New Orleans on September 7 for the beginning of oral testimony. In addition to the Original Knights of the Ku Klux Klan as an organization, thirty-five local members or presumed sympathizers were named as individuals.

Once the injunctive suit had been filed and the federal court orders issued, there was a noticeable difference in the racial climate in the city. It almost seemed as though the town was waiting for something good to come of it—perhaps, eventually, a solution.

Blacks scheduled a night march for Thursday, August 5, following two daytime marches on August 3 and 4. But the night march was called off after Judge Christenberry talked with attorneys for the city and the local Blacks.

On August 6, President Johnson signed the nation's new Voting Rights Act of 1965, ensuring the right to vote by all citizens of the United States, regardless of the color of their skin. The day before, the Crown Zellerbach Corporation, owner of the paper mill that was Bogalusa's one and only large industry and by far the largest employer, announced that it was complying with the civil rights law of the land.

A few more days passed before the Voters League and City officials held talks again on Tuesday, August 10. There was no march, there were no pickets. Talks were set again for the following Saturday.

Meanwhile, Black residents—as a result of the new voting rights law—swarmed to the Registrar of Voters office at the Washington Parish courthouse in Franklinton to sign up to vote. Between August 11 and 17, there were nearly 350 new registered voters in the parish, almost all of them Black.

While no pickets were out on the street on August 10 and 11, they were again in front of downtown businesses on August 12. A few pickets continued to show up daily, but the numbers had dwindled and the momentum seemed to be fading. But a white womens' "civilian patrol" was announced, its purpose being to watch for harassment of white women going to stores where Blacks were picketing.

August 17 was a big "Bonus Days" retail promotion in town, and merchants reported good crowds turning out for bargains. There were still only a handful of Black pickets and nobody paid them any attention.

The governor got back into the picture a week later by naming a forty-two-member Louisiana Race Relations Committee of twenty-one whites and twenty-one Blacks from across the state. It was incredulous that, after all of the racial tension and violence in Bogalusa during the previous months, not one member of the committee was from Bogalusa or Washington Parish. There were many people from Bogalusa who could surely have been very helpful to the committee by virtue of their experiences of the past several months.

Schools were set to open—including the court-ordered integration of grades 1 and 12—in just a few days, and the sultry days of late August were the calm before the storm.

On Wednesday, September 1, three Black students attended Bogalusa High School for the first time in history, and there were no problems. Two first-graders also attended Columbia Street Elementary School that day without incident.

The next day, however, trouble erupted at a drive-up ice cream stand on Columbia Street. There was a brawl involving some older teenagers.

Two days later, at 5:30 p.m. on Saturday, September 4, fighting broke out again, this time on East 4th Street, where white hecklers followed Black pickets who had left their posts in front of the stores on Columbia

Street. Shots were fired, but nobody was hit. More arrests of both races were made.

On Monday, September 6, some 2,000 whites took part in a motorcade from downtown to the Bogalusa airport on the north side of town for a rally. Among the rallyers again was District Judge John Rarick from St. Francisville, always in the forefront now as a staunch "states-righter." Back downtown that day, about 150 Blacks walked to the gates of the Crown Zellerbach paper mill to picket the plant, charging job discrimination.

All of that commotion took place the day before the court hearing on the federal government's suit against the Ku Klux Klan was to open in New Orleans. Seventy-one people were sworn in on that opening day of the trial.

I had been served a civil subpoena to testify on Wednesday, September 8, and was ordered to bring with me "copies of all Klan material you have received and copies of all editorials dealing with the Ku Klux Klan" that had run in the paper.

Assembling that much material in such a short time would have been overwhelming; when I asked for additional time, my personal appearance in court was determined to be unnecessary, and the court allowed material previously submitted to the FBI to be used.

Testimony continued all week long in the federal court building in New Orleans, and the battling in Bogalusa seemed to stand still. The segregationists were getting daily reports from New Orleans, waiting to see what was going to happen before causing more problems for the Black people at home. At the same time, the Black protestors also seemed to stand down, waiting to see what would result from the federal assault in the courts.

During that week, though, Hurricane Betsy had rounded the Florida peninsula and moved through the Gulf of Mexico on a northwesterly track. Bogalusans and all other south Louisiana residents of both races had watched warily and prepared. Late on Thursday, September 9, and into the next day, the storm swept just east of New Orleans and swamped parts of New Orleans and the parishes south and east of the city. Bogalusa and Washington Parish were relatively unscathed by a glancing blow.

On Sunday, September 19, Reverend Bruce Shepherd, who had seen St. Matthew's Episcopal Church bitterly divided over the race issue, announced his resignation from the pulpit. Reverend Shepherd had battled his adversaries openly and with dignity for a very long time, but the division within his church had cost it not only members, but also revenues. His foes had stooped to some nasty false accusations about Reverend Shepherd which helped sooth their consciences at withholding their tithes. A whisper campaign continued the Klan's earlier Midnight Mail accusations about his excessive drinking and the fact that he had befriended a homeless young man. Bruce, being a bachelor priest, was an easy target. In a small country town like Bogalusa, small-town gossip could often be deadly.

Several weeks after the cancellation of the Hays meeting, Reverend Shepherd had been quoted in the *Wall Street Journal* as urging his small flock of Episcopalians to "help overcome the evil which is rampant in our city—the things going on here are unbelievable." But without full support from even his own congregation, he felt his moving on would be in the best interest of St. Matthew's Parish, and he told the church that he was resigning to take a position as chaplain at Duke University in Durham, North Carolina, and would assume his new post a month later. He served the on-campus Episcopal flock there until his death in 1979 at the age of sixty-five.

I felt his leaving Bogalusa was a distinct loss for the city and it was for me personally. But his assessment of the move on his part was no doubt correct. One by one, the six men who had hoped to bring racial peace to Bogalusa with the Brooks Hays invitation were being forced to leave the city. The two Baptist ministers—Reverend Jerry Chance at Main Street Baptist Church and Reverend Paul G. Gillespie at Memorial Baptist—had gone. Radio station WBOX owner Ralph Blumberg was gone. Now the Episcopal priest was leaving. Only attorney Bascom Talley and I were still in the city from among that Brooks Hays "Committee of Six."

The exodus of the four people who had sought a peaceful resolution to racial strife in Bogalusa demonstrated the ugly truth: the Ku Klux Klan and its supporters were strong forces intent on blocking integration in Bogalusa and Washington Parish. But more blocks continued to fall with the September 29 order that the Washington-St. Tammany Charity Hospital, a state institution, be desegregated, and with the October 13 court order that the Washington Parish School System join the city schools in integrating their classrooms.

In addition to the court action in New Orleans and the skirmishes in Bogalusa, "The Fair" was coming up. The huge and renowned Washington Parish Free Fair—which has long billed itself as the "Largest Free Fair in the Nation"—is held in the parish seat of Franklinton every Wednesday through Saturday during the third week in October. Traditionally, Black visitors did not attend during the first three days, and Saturday had always been designated as "Colored Day" at the Fair.

In the advent of the 1965 Fair, a new hate group name popped up for delivery of the Midnight Mail—the Knights of the White Camellia. Their Midnight Mail lamented changes they saw coming to "their"—the whites'—Fair: "What is to happen to our Fair? A Fair that has become a tradition, built by the white people of Washington Parish over a period of a half century."

The flyer went on to name and criticize local officials for cooperating (or at least not fighting?) with the court-ordered integration of the four-day fall harvest festival: "Not one word has been said on the white people's behalf" by (State) Representative Lawrence "Buster" Sheridan, (State) Senator B. B. "Sixty" Rayburn, Washington Parish Sheriff Dorman Crowe, US Congressman Jimmie Morrison, Louisiana Governor John McKeithen, and 22nd District Attorney W. W. "Squinch" Erwin.

I found it odd that US Senators Allen Ellender and Russell Long, both powerful figures in Congress, weren't part of the Knights' "rogue's gallery."

So at that year's fair, some Blacks did break the "tradition" and they attended—without incident—during the first three days, and then almost totally boycotted the event on Saturday. The fairgrounds, normally jammed with huge crowds of thousands, was eerily deserted on Fair Saturday that year. This was the beginning of the eventual total restructuring of the four-day parish fair programming. It gave whites an extra day to attend, on Saturday, and it gave Blacks *three* more days of the fair.

The Black community, during the weekend of the fair, also molded a powerful school boycott. On Monday morning after the fair, October 18, nearly 1,500 Black students in the Bogalusa schools boycotted classes. Hundreds had skipped school the prior Wednesday when they went to Franklinton to integrate the fair. And all schools were closed for the fair on Thursday and Friday. So the Black boycott on Monday was not totally unexpected.

It had been widely expected that there would be disciplinary action on Monday for those who skipped to go to the opening day of the fair on the previous Wednesday, but with attendance of Blacks down 62 percent, discipline was avoided.

Instead of going to school on Monday morning, the Black student boycotters marched to the Bogalusa City School Board office, singing "We shall overcome." When they arrived at the school headquarters, they presented a list of demands.

What they asked for were more qualified teachers, another foreign language in the curriculum, new books and laboratory equipment, a full-time physician at every school, building repairs and remodeling, and action on complaints previously filed with the system. It was an ambitious wish list, one which the school system could never have afforded financially even if it were inclined to meet the demands.

Black student absenteeism in Bogalusa, at 1,455 on Monday, held steady at 1,424 on Tuesday. On Wednesday, police offered the students an alternate route for their march to the school board office on Cumberland Street because of barricades for street construction work. But the students refused the alternate route, and when they also refused to disperse upon police orders, seventy-three were arrested for disturbing the peace and failing to move on.

The students were taken to the city jail, where they immediately clogged the drains. Police cut off the water and a CORE attorney immediately accused the police of denying the prisoners use of water. Police said they would turn the water back on if the students would not clog the drains. That was agreed to—but as soon as the water was turned back on, the students again blocked the drain and the water was once again shut off to keep the jail from flooding.

In addition to the seventy-three student marchers arrested that day, another twenty-one were arrested at the police headquarters for blocking the driveway. None of them had a parade or march permit.

The students were let out on bond and by the following Monday, October 25, Black student attendance in the schools was much closer to normal. There were 335 absent that day, far down from nearly 1,500 the previous Monday, and at 13 percent only a blip above the normal 10 percent absenteeism rate.

In the midst of the Black school boycott came the opening of hearings in Washington, DC, by the Congressional House Committee on Un-American Activities. Thirteen weeks of testimony about Ku Klux Klan activities across the nation, especially in the Deep South, was anticipated.

The list of area Klan units targeted for investigation by the committee included The Original Knights of the Ku Klux Klan, Washington Parish, Bogalusa, Varnado, and Bush; the Bush Hunting Club; and Fishing Club No. 1055. A number of Bogalusa area men had been subpoenaed to testify when the committee's questioning was to focus on Klan activity in Bogalusa and Washington Parish.

With the current field of racial action being the courts of the land and the US Congress, little of great moment was taking place in Bogalusa—everyone was waiting to see what the three-judge federal court in New Orleans was going to do as a result of the September hearings.

That's why a march on Thanksgiving Day through Bogalusa to a deserted City Hall by 130 Blacks was a surprise. There was virtually nobody out to watch and City Hall was closed, so, once done, the marchers returned uneventfully to their homes.

On Halloween night, a Sunday, the "King Kleagle" of the New York Klan shot himself to death at the home of the KKK leader in neighboring Pennsylvania. It was a bewildering incident, but almost nothing more than a footnote to history in terms of national news coverage.

Before the judges from New Orleans could hand down their ruling against the Klan, Representative Charles L. Weltner of Georgia made a scathing public attack on the Bogalusa Klan in a speech on the floor of the House of Representatives, and he had it inserted into the Congressional Record of the 89th Congress with the title "The Terror of Bogalusa: A Case in Point."

Representative Weltner—who was one of the panelists on the House subcommittee that was probing the Klan—placed the blame for Bogalusa's racial troubles on public officials who had failed early on to perform their duties. He noted the city's nickname as "The Magic City," and continued, "Unfortunately, the Klan has stripped away most of the magic and cast over it a pall that will endure for some years to come."

Representative Weltner named various members of the Klan and detailed their positions as friends and neighbors of city officials and as members of city government, including the police and fire departments. He also noted the Klan's "long siege of harassment" against Ralph Blumberg and his radio station and against the *Daily News* and me for "burning crosses on the owner's lawn, puncturing his automobile tires, and abusing him in unsigned letters and scurrilous circulars." It would have been nice if I actually had been the owner of the paper as Representative Weltner credited to me, but I was merely the publisher. The owners, the brothers Wick, were far away in Arizona and Washington, DC.

Representative Weltner's insertion into the Congressional Record also publicly listed 175 Bogalusa area men as members of the Klan.

"Mr. Speaker, I now place into the Record the names of members of the Ku Klux Klan of Bogalusa and the Anti-Communist Christian Association. These names are derived from Federal Court records, as submitted pursuant to court order."

The list contained the names of many men I knew to be Klansmen, many I did not, and many men I didn't know at all.

After submitting the list of names to the House Speaker for publication in the Congressional Record, Representative Weltner said:

> I place these names before the public so the public may know with whom it deals. I fully believe that full information, amply imparted to the public, will be an adequate remedy. Now, when a decent citizen receives a threatening telephone call, he has an idea who might be calling. When he finds the now familiar leaflet, "The KKK Is Watching You" in his mailbox, he will know who is watching. When he finds a sticker proclaiming "Your Neighbor Is a Klansman," he can now judge the truth of that matter.

I had received a complimentary letter from a newspaper publisher in Texas that fall. He had subscribed to the *Daily News* because, as a newspaperman, he felt during a visit to Bogalusa that he had a "sympathetic understanding" of the *Daily News*'s challenges during difficult times, so he wanted to follow the situation for a while.

"From contact with some of your citizens and through reading your newspaper," he wrote, "I have come to feel that not only is your community well served by its newspaper, but also your local law enforcement agencies have conducted themselves in a commendable manner in dealing with a most complex and difficult problem . . . In closing let me commend you on an unusually well edited and otherwise interesting newspaper of daily circulation."

I had sent the letter on to *Daily News* majority owner Milt Wick, who had called me to Washington during the summer to talk about the Klan, conservatism, and the role of the newspaper in the community. On November 9, Wick responded, on *Human Events* letterhead, writing that the letter from a fellow newspaper publisher was "a wonderful commentary on how well you have handled your many news problems during the past 10 months of racial disturbance. I am returning your letter herewith. It should serve as a memento of the era—something you should preserve forever as evidence of your tact, effectiveness and judgment."

One man named by the courts and the House Un-American Activities

Committee went to a Notary in November to disclaim affiliation with the Klan. He swore that he had never been and was not now a member of the Klan or any of its affiliated organizations. This was an option open to everybody named, but no one else chose to follow his lead.

Words of wisdom—or perhaps concern—were coming now from many sources as street battles seemed to be on hold.

In a letter to me, one of the city's Black moderates wrote me to challenge one statement in the "A Time for Optimism" editorial. He said, in part:

> At one point in the article you referred to the necessity of the Negro community realizing its responsibilities. You went on to indict the entire Negro community for damaging Bogalusa by picketing and marching. Your statement is no more unfair than it would be for me to say that the white community should realize its responsibilities, and that it has done enough harm with its cross burnings, harassments and other lawless acts. You know I believe that the moderates of both races have not been led forward in this community, and that we have lacked civic, political and industrial leadership . . .
>
> I believe that you are basically interested in a better community. I hope you will receive this in a spirit of friendly criticism and will not print blanket indictments of the Negro Community in the future.

Mayor Cutrer received a note of encouragement from Executive Secretary of the Commission on Religion and Race J. Frederick McKirachan, citing the mayor's public reversal in the race issue:

> The Commission on Religion and Race of the United Presbyterian Synod of Pennsylvania commends you for promising repeal of all segregation ordinances in your city and for pledging employment of Negroes in departments of your city government. In this time of national tension and unrest your action is a significant stride forward and represents a quality of leadership sensitive to the moral dimension and demands of

our time. If we may serve or assist you in any way, please call upon us. Your decision may bring you under attack and place you in the lonely position of a voice crying in the wilderness. Be assured you are not without friends and supporters. Warmest regards.

A Black local businessman wrote a letter to the manager of the paper mill seeking help in getting a truly biracial committee named in Bogalusa. Heaven knows there were enough committees; it was just that they were all either totally Black or totally white, but, speaking for the Black community, the businessman wrote, in part:

> We are convinced that the only way to remove the deep seated resentments and dissatisfaction in the Negro Community is to create some bi-racial commission or committee, with regular meetings, whose function would be to openly discuss problems between the races. We believe that the Bogalusa Voters League, the Schools, Unions, Churches, and other Negro Civic Groups should be represented . . .
>
> We are convinced that the best contribution Crown Zellerbach can make is to use its influence on the City Administration to create such a committee. If this fails, then we feel that Crown Zellerbach should join with us in such a movement, in spite of the City Administration. This procedure has proved helpful when elected officials have failed to act in other southern cities.

The September hearings in the suit against the Klan in Federal Court in New Orleans finally yielded momentous results on Wednesday, December 1. The three-judge panel condemned Klansman as "bullies who exploit the forces of hate, prejudice and ignorance," and announced that the court would soon issue an injunction against the Klan in Bogalusa. The judges accused the Klan of "ineradicable evil of violence, intimidation and coercion in Washington Parish."

While the announcement did not put an end to Ku Klux Klan activity in Bogalusa and the parish—note the characterization of the Klan's "evil of violence" as ineradicable—it did send thunder through the ranks and had a chilling effect.

The judges, whose opinion was written by Judge John Minor Wisdom and concurred with by Judges Herbert Christenberry and John Ainsworth, said that the thirty-two named defendants were supposed to be leaders of the community. "Instead, they appear to be ignorant bullies, callous of the harm they know they are doing and lacking in sufficient understanding to comprehend the chasm between their own twisted Konstitution and the noble charter of liberties under the law that is the American Constitution."

The judges added that the Klan tried to make it appear that it no longer existed by using the "respectable title" of "Anti-Communist Christian Crusade." They called that a "sham." As organized, though, the Anti-Communist Christians were an association, not a crusade.

Three weeks later, on Wednesday, December 22, the federal injunction was formally issued against the Ku Klux Klan and the thirty-two men who had been named as defendants. After the hearings ended, there was a welcome calm throughout the city and parish. The Black community had made enormous gains and the Klan was brought to its knees.

From that date on, the KKK, or the ACCC (Anti-Communist Christian Crusade), was walking on eggshells. It was not the end of Klan activity in Bogalusa and Washington Parish, but there was a new national stigma attached to them and all they stood for. To people who believed in law and order and the dignity of man, it was a wondrous Christmas present.

During Christmas week of 1965, the "United Klans of America" announced it would hold a rally on Friday, December 26, in Bogalusa and one on Saturday, December 27, across the Pearl River in Crossroads, Mississippi. The UKA said the rallies would feature "America's Most Courageous Patriot," Robert M. Shelton, Imperial Wizard of the United Klans of America, Inc., Knights of the Ku Klux Klan." The flyer was printed with an address in Alexandria, Louisiana, but it was also stamped with an address about thirty miles south of Bogalusa, in Covington in neighboring St. Tammany Parish.

The day after the Klan's rallies, CORE's militant national director, James Farmer, announced on Sunday, December 28, that he would resign his position on March 1 of the following year to head a new government-private organization on education for the poor. It was a belated Christmas present for those who were critical of Farmer and CORE's tactics under his leadership.

Farmer, after leaving CORE, later taught at Lincoln University in Oxford, Pennsylvania, before serving as assistant secretary of Health, Education, and Welfare in the administration of President Richard Nixon. He then taught at the University of Mary Washington and died in Fredericksburg, Virginia, in 1999 at age 79. He said of his days of organizing civil rights protests in the Deep South: "Anyone who said he wasn't afraid during the civil rights movement was either a liar or without imagination. I think we were all scared. I was scared all the time. My hands didn't shake but inside I was shaking."

11

BLUMBERG IS A LIAR

1966

The year 1966 dawned with subpoenas for more several Bogalusa-area men to appear before the House Committee on Un-American Activities, which had resumed its Klan investigation hearings in Washington, DC, following a year-end holiday break. Six of the dozen or so area residents called to Washington to testify, however, were among the group already under injunction by the federal court. Almost all of the local men who sat before the panel were accompanied by the same Baton Rouge attorney.

"Taking the Fifth" became a familiar refrain at the hearings. One by one, the local men testifying at the hearings didn't actually testify—they invoked their Fifth Amendment right against self-incrimination.

Along the way through the hearings, the committee chairman, Representative Edwin Willis—himself a Louisianian from Arnaudville in St. Landry Parish—informed the men being questioned that until they availed themselves of the opportunity to confirm, deny, or refute any of the details of the committee's questioning, then those facts would be assumed to be true. Put simply: say it ain't so, or it's so.

Still, they took the Fifth.

On the second day after the hearings resumed, on January 5, former Bogalusa radio station owner Ralph Blumberg, a member of the Hays "Committee of Six" who had since left town, offered up his self-serving testimony before the House Committee, and it stunned me. I had thought initially that the newspaper would not respond to some of

Blumberg's testimony, but after reading what he told the committee on Wednesday and considering it overnight, I did respond with a page-one editorial on Thursday, January 6, and I titled it as bluntly as I could.

BLUMBERG IS A LIAR

For most of yesterday afternoon and this morning, this newspaper thought it best to ignore statements made in Washington, DC, yesterday by Ralph Blumberg, who used to operate a radio station here. But there are times when it becomes necessary to call a spade a spade.

Yesterday before the House Un-American Activities Committee in Washington, Ralph Blumberg lied.

He apparently enjoyed the limelight and made statements pertaining to the *Daily News* which are not true. We do not intend to discuss all of the other things he said before the committee, but the statements he made about this newspaper shall not go unchallenged.

Blumberg was quoted as saying "the *Bogalusa Daily News* publishes news slanted the way the Klan wants it slanted."

There is no nice way of putting it: Blumberg is a liar.

This newspaper prints both sides of issues and slants its news in no direction. We print the news and let the people make up their own minds.

This short editorial will never find its way into the Congressional Record like Blumberg's diatribe in Washington, but we feel that Blumberg should know that along with his so-called "fight for freedom of speech" goes a responsibility for telling the truth, a point which he has obviously forgotten.

Before making the charge that the *Daily News* slanted its coverage to the Klan's liking, Blumberg had told the committee, "At this time the newspaper, which was formerly a liberal paper, is a completely conservative newspaper. It is not the real policy of the editor down there. It isn't what he really believes."

And then, ". . . but, unfortunately, the Klan has won their battle in Bogalusa. They control, they influence now all of the press, the news media."

Blumberg's statements were really unexpected by me. I do know that when he left Bogalusa, there were no goodbyes or good luck—not to me, anyway. The only reason I can think that Blumberg would testify as he did was to somehow show, to his way of thinking, that the only way somebody could survive in the communications field in Bogalusa—as he had not been able to do—was to bow to the wishes of the Ku Klux Klan.

The *Daily News* proved unequivocally that this was not true. Blumberg, at one point during the days when his station was being boycotted, actually met with Klan members. What took place nobody ever knew. But there was no way that I, as publisher of the *Daily News*, would meet with KKK members—even at the height of their campaign against the paper, our subscribers and advertisers, and me and my family.

In March 1965, Blumberg had told the *New York Times* in an interview, "You have to live here to believe this. But we're not crusaders, we're not heroes, and we don't want to be martyrs. We just don't want to be run out of town with our tails between our legs."

Yet Blumberg *was* run out of business and decided to leave town, and it is a pity. But it was cowardly of him to try to justify the failure of his business by pointing an undeserved finger at the *Daily News* in his testimony to the US Congress.

Blumberg had bought WBOX in 1961. After he left town in 1965 without so much as a goodbye to me, he received the Paul White Award from the Radio and Television Digital News Association. In his acceptance speech, he said, "When you become a target of the Ku Klux Klan you soon learn that if ever there was a devil on the face of the earth, it lives, breathes, it functions in the cloaked evil of the leaders of the Ku Klux Klan. And you cannot compromise with the devil."

I sympathize with Blumberg for what he went through in Bogalusa, and I commend him for that and other awards he won during his radio career. But as far as his comment about the *Daily News* goes, it wasn't an award-winning performance that Blumberg put on in the Congressional chambers—at least not in my opinion. After a long career in radio in other parts of the country, Blumberg died at age 79 in 2002, back in his native area of St. Louis.

Black protesters were back on Columbia Street on Saturday, January 29, with a march and demonstrations, but there were no incidents. It appeared that the clamp put on the Klan by the Federal Court in New Orleans was making itself felt. The court's continued warning that local police had better provide proper protection for the demonstrators was also having its effect.

With everything having noticeably cooled down in the city, on Monday, February 14, attorney John Martzell of New Orleans, who had been hired by the City of Bogalusa to help with its negotiations with Black residents and with the city's defense in suits brought by them, was named director of the State of Louisiana's Human Relations Commission. "We all learned the high cost of bad race relations," he said. Summing up the Bogalusa situation, Martzell said, "that problem somehow defies description."

After the federal court ruling in New Orleans, events began to be more spread-out in time—consequential events were no longer occurring on a daily basis. Pickets weren't in front of the stores every day; daily rallies were not being held. There were no more marches on City Hall. Was it all over?

But on Thursday, March 10, Black Army Captain Donald Ray Sims of Bogalusa, home on leave, was shot at 1:20 a.m. while he was inside a pay telephone booth on Columbia Street. The twenty-nine-year-old captain was shot from a distance of only three to four feet, but he said his assailant must have come up from behind because he did not see him.

Two days later, Bogalusa police arrested a white man and charged him with attempted murder. The man had seen Captain Sims in the phone booth and went his way. But an hour later he passed by and saw Captain Sims still in the phone booth and shot a .22 caliber pistol four times through the glass window of the phone booth. One of the shots hit Captain Sims in the shoulder. Captain Sims returned to duty with the Army. After two delays, the man who allegedly shot him was never brought to trial.

Robert Hicks, vice-president of the Voters League, announced on Monday, March 28, that Black marches would resume the next day. He said they would be held daily thereafter until Blacks' grievances were addressed. The demands included the firing of a Washington Parish Sheriff's deputy whom Blacks consistently accused of brutality. Also demanded was the solution of Deputy Oneal Moore's murder.

Floyd McKissick, succeeding James Farmer as the new national director of CORE, led the Tuesday afternoon march to City Hall. Nearly 200 Blacks took part in the march, most of them teenagers. There were no incidents.

On Wednesday, March 30, Voters League leaders met with Mayor Cutrer and presented a new list of demands—this one more extensive than those presented earlier. They demanded that Cutrer act as mediator in many areas, including fighting poverty among Blacks, welfare, security, housing, streets, sidewalks, hospital matters, opening city parks to all, and a centrally located public library. They also demanded one-third Black representation on the Bogalusa Police Department to mirror their share of the city's population. The street march that day was again about 200 people, and again almost all of them were youths.

A. Z. Young said the Voters League was again planning to hold night marches, even though they had been banned by the city. Young also threatened to call in the dreaded Black Muslims to Bogalusa if local Blacks' demands were not met. Charles Evers, field director for the NAACP, urged a boycott of all white businesses in the city.

The rhetoric was definitely being heated up again by Black leadership—but there was no retaliation reaction by the whites. As a matter of fact, another significant change took place the following day, on April 1. All Bogalusa motels were "officially" opened up to Black guests. It was accomplished rather quietly, with nothing more than a short story announcing the change on page one of that day's *Daily News*.

The Voters League had scheduled a night march for that Saturday,

April 2. Hicks said the night march would be held even if it was against the law, but he stipulated that it would be held only if 200 Blacks showed up to take part and were willing to be arrested by police. At 7:30 that night, only 129 Blacks were on hand at the usual starting place on Columbia Street. Police Chief Claxton Knight was there, and warned them that they would be arrested if they marched in defiance of the ban on night marches. The crowd dissipated and the downtown streets were left empty.

Across the state line just east of the Pearl River, however, a "United Conservatives" rally was being held in Crossroads, Mississippi, and it drew a large crowd.

On Wednesday, April 6, A. Z. Young and Charles Sims, from the Voters League and the Deacons for Defense, were in Chicago organizing a Chicago Deacons for Defense—and trying to raise money for the defense of the Black Bogalusa school students who had boycotted their classes, flooded the city jail, and then been charged with delinquency.

A bizarre incident occurred on Monday afternoon, April 30. FBI agents had been telephoning the house of a man in the city's Terrace neighborhood. They wanted to ask some questions relating to the murder of Deputy Moore and the shooting of his partner Creed Rogers.

The man answered the door and fired a shot into the ground at their feet. The FBI agents left, but they returned that night and were greeted by a sign the man had hastily erected on his front lawn following the afternoon encounter: "No Trespassing—Agents, Peddlers, Salesmen, Visitors, Reporters. Call Before Entering." But there were no reports of a violent encounter.

It was high irony that the current issue of *Newsweek* magazine reported that Brooks Hays—by then serving as assistant director of the federal Community Relations Service and the man who Governor McKeithen had told to "stay out" of Louisiana when we invited him to speak in Bogalusa in early 1965—had been named an "Honorary Colonel" on McKeithen's staff. Time has a way of changing so many things.

A trial in May 1966 was held for a man charged with assaulting an FBI agent in Bogalusa in 1965. A mistrial was declared in the case when the jury told the federal court judge in New Orleans that it was "hopelessly deadlocked." A new trial was held in September and the jury found him guilty. He was sentenced to a year in federal prison.

There was more shooting in Bogalusa during the early part of 1966. On April 16, shots were fired into a house; on May 13, shots were fired into the Acme Cafe on Columbia Street at 1:00 a.m. It was thought that these incidents involved Blacks who were not happy with other Blacks' cooperation with the local civil rights effort.

During that summer in 1966, as civil rights related street battles raged in New York City, Cleveland, Baltimore, and Jonesville, Louisiana, violence between Blacks and whites had seemed to disappear from the streets of Bogalusa.

And the Klan was still active elsewhere in the state.

On July 19, 1966, Victor Bussie's home in Baton Rouge was bombed by suspected Klansmen who were no friends of the Louisiana labor leader. Bussie, who had been jeered and heckled on the Columbia Street sidewalk when he arrived to speak to the Rotary Club in October 1963, was a fireman who had risen through the ranks of the Shreveport firefighters' union, became president of the Louisiana AFL-CIO in 1956, and remained the unopposed leader of the state's largest labor union for the next four decades.

But Bussie's visits to Bogalusa and other civil rights hotspots in Louisiana had made him a pariah to the KKK. He was a "liberal" Democrat in a time when there weren't many Republicans in the state and many of the Democrats were far more conservative than he was. During the 1960s, his civil rights work and his support for President Lyndon Johnson led not only to the bombing of his home, but also to a 40-percent decline in AFL-CIO membership in the state. Bussie was enshrined into the second class of the Louisiana Political Museum and Hall in Fame in 1994, and he died in 2011 at the age of 92.

Though it may have seemed so, all was not quiet in Bogalusa. In addition to the shootings into the Acme Cafe and the local home, another Black man was murdered in the city. Clarence Triggs, a twenty-four-year-old bricklayer who had moved to Bogalusa a year earlier and who had attended local protest meetings and demonstrations, was found shot to death on Saturday night, July 30, in a wrecked car at the busy intersection of North Columbia Street and Louisiana Avenue. The car was registered in the name of a white Bogalusa man's wife. The woman's husband and another man were arrested and charged with Triggs's murder and were later indicted by a Washington Parish Grand Jury. The husband was never brought to trial, and the man with him went to trial and was acquitted.

Triggs's name is engraved on the plaza memorial, along with that of slain Deputy Sheriff Oneal Moore, at the Civil Rights Memorial Center in Montgomery, Alabama.

As the new 1966–67 school term was beginning, black-white confrontations were on tap. The most serious problem was again at Bogalusa Junior High, which had been moved into the former all-black Central Memorial High School building adjacent to downtown and two blocks from the *Daily News* offices. On Monday, September 12, Black and white students cursed one another and traded insults, but there were no serious fights.

The same thing happened the next day at the same school. By Thursday, September 22, similar events had spread to the Bogalusa High School campus across town, and Black students boycotted classes while demanding and awaiting a court order for protection from white students. The next day, six white students were placed under court order to stop assaulting and intimidating Black students.

Archconservatives in the area got a big boost when avowed segregationist Judge John Rarick pulled a political upset of monumental proportions at the polls. Rarick defeated incumbent James H. "Jimmy" Morrison in a Democratic runoff (there wasn't much of a Republican presence in the state at that time) for the US House of Representatives seat that Morrison of Hammond had held for twenty-four years.

Rarick won by 85,330 to 81,551 votes, a fairly close margin. But in Bogalusa, he out-polled Morrison by nearly a two-to-one margin, 4,851 to 2,544. One thing was certain: if Rarick received any Black votes in Bogalusa or Washington Parish—it was only because the wrong voting machine lever had been pulled. It was a staggering defeat for all moderates on the racial issue.

Earlier that summer, a new newspaper had finally appeared in Bogalusa. The first edition of the *Bogalusa American* came out on June 16, 1966, just in time to heavily support Rarick's run for Congress.

The *American*, which came out weekly, promoted itself as Bogalusa's home-owned newspaper because the *Daily News* was majority-owned by the Wick brothers' Arizona-based company. The *American's* pages were filled with political commentary—mostly written by national conservative columnists, some locally written sports and commentary columns, usually a page one article about some local citizen of note, a few other local photos and stories, and a lot of "filler." The paper had little to no coverage of local government—City Hall, the city School Board, or the Parish Police Jury (County Board of Supervisors)—to provide its readers routine coverage on matters that could affect their lives as citizens of the community. It was mostly a vehicle for archconservative commentary and no real competition for the *Daily News*.

But because that summer was the campaign season for the fall congressional elections, many editions of the *American* seemed to be little more than a campaign publication for Judge Rarick. The archconservative segregationist was prominently featured on the front page of many issues from the *American's* start-up in early summer until the congressional campaign in November.

But after the 1966 congressional election in November and the holiday shopping season in December, the *American* fell on hard times. The paper never generated enough advertising or subscribers to break even, and less than a year after it was started, the *Daily News* was the instrument of its death. We had the *Daily News's* insurance agent make a "blind" third-party purchase-offer to the people connected to the *American*. The offer—less than a thousand dollars!—was quickly accepted.

One issue that was ready to press was still published by the previous owners after the sale was closed, but then we closed the paper down, and that was when the *American's* backers found out that they had actually sold it to the newspaper that they so hated. The Midnight Mail howled at the loss of a "true conservative" paper, and took Bascom Talley, the insurance agent, and me to task in their typically impolite terms. The life of the *American* ran from early summer of 1966 to early spring of 1967. The single green-covered volume containing most of a year's worth of bound copies of the weekly paper became *Daily News* property and are still part of the *Daily News*'s archives.

A few more federal court rulings were in the offing the latter part of 1966, all of which, oddly enough, could be labeled "pro-white." On November 1, Judge Christenberry dismissed a contempt of court suit filed by Black residents against Bogalusa Police Chief Claxton Knight and Captain Haynes "Twister" Wascom. The judge found that the two police officials had not failed to carry out the edicts of the court.

A week later, a man charged with planning to burn the Black Ebenezer Baptist Church was acquitted due to lack of evidence. That same night, however, the same man was back in the Bogalusa jail on a charge of disturbing the peace by fighting in a Bogalusa shopping center parking lot.

On November 17, a Washington Parish sheriff's deputy was cleared in federal court on a charge that he had beaten two Black men.

Politics had been in the air for several months and the big news— other than Judge Rarick's stunning defeat of Congressman Morrison— was that Mayor Cutrer had decided he'd had enough and would not run for another term at Bogalusa City Hall. Succeeding him and taking the oath of office as Bogalusa mayor on Monday, December 5, 1966, was WIKC radio station owner Curt Siegelin.

Siegelin had earlier served as mayor of Bogalusa before resigning in midterm to take an appointive job with state government. But he decided to return to Bogalusa, and because he had been a popular mayor during his earlier terms, it was no surprise that he made the comeback to succeed Cutrer. He was also viewed as a racial moderate and possibly as someone to help calm the racially troubled waters of the city in the latter years of the 1960s.

Testimony before the House Un-American Activities Committee, which had begun on October 19, 1965, had concluded on February 24, 1966. But from the end of the hearings until December 11, 1967, work had continued on compiling the committee's report. The report was six gray-covered softbound volumes filled with testimony and documentation by, of, and about the Ku Klux Klan in the United States.

The collection was an exhaustive study of the Klan and all of its fragmentations in the country. A considerable portion of it dealt with the Original Knights of the Ku Klux Klan, which was Louisiana's version of the KKK. Investigations by the House proved that the Original Knights had dissolved in mid-1965, when various factions within the organization began to disagree over leadership and money.

In Bogalusa, the immediate successor to the Original Knights of the Ku Klux Klan was the ACCC—the Anti-Communist Christian Crusade—which had actually incorporated in Louisiana in December 1964, before the breakup of the Original Knights. But as 1965 wore on, that splinter group was replaced by the United Klans of America, Inc. (UKA).

A number of Bogalusa and Washington Parish-area Klansmen were identified in the House Committee's report, although none of them had testified as to their membership, upholding the Klan's oath of secrecy by "taking the Fifth."

The House report is both fascinating and sickening. The detail of Klan activities across the country, principally in the South, and specifically in Bogalusa and Washington Parish and in neighboring St. Tammany Parish to the south and nearby Mississippi to the north and east, is a story of unabated hate, terrorism, and intimidation.

Unlike the court action in New Orleans, the House hearings were designed to produce information about the Ku Klux Klan in America for use by the Congress in formulating legislation to ensure that the nation's laws on equal rights would not be subverted. The six-volume set is a long-unwinding story dealing primarily with hate and intimidation and, in part, with the struggles of whites and Blacks in a small Southern paper mill town trying to find their way out of a hall of shame.

12

HAS THE KLAN STORY REALLY ENDED?

1967 and Beyond

The Midnight Mail continued to hit driveways and sidewalks in 1967 and into 1968 and 1969. The droppings occasionally hit on the old racial themes, but they tended to focus more on local politics and tax issues. Mayor Curt Siegelin, who had succeeded Jesse Cutrer at the beginning of the year, and Bogalusa School Superintendent Moise Israel were both slurred in several Midnight Mails when city and the school system each asked voters to approve tax measures at the polls. City councilmen and administrators were blasted over issues of governance, including efforts to pass an ordinance banning the midnight mails—which would have been impossible to enforce. There's no way of knowing who was behind any given "mail." It is possible that it was not the original Klansmen of previous years tossing those rolled flyers, but others who were merely copying the by-then very familiar form of anonymous community commentary to grind their own axes. But some of the throw-outs did claim to be from the KKK, while others did not. Some even included potshots at the authors and issues in previous flyers.

On July 21, a letter marked "Personal" came to me at the paper. It was anonymous in effect, because it was signed by the "KKK's." It read:

> It has been brought to the attention of the Klan that the paper boys putting out the *Daily News* are asked to pick up all the Klan literature that has been flying around. The Klan doesn't destroy the papers of the *Daily News* and it is certainly wrong to destroy something that doesn't

concern the individual, etc. If my son worked for a place that taught such principles—he would quit and the firm would be exposed. This is being checked into and I sincerely hope this rumor isn't correct. You are in the position to check and stop this if it is going on before someone gets into serious trouble.

My reaction was: (1) I didn't ask our carriers to do such a thing, (2) if I had, why would I check and stop it, and (3) anyone who was taking that stuff off the streets would be performing a public service.

That summer there were more marches, but they were not limited to cross-town processions to Bogalusa City Hall.

On July 23, 1967, more than 100 marchers led by A. Z. Young, Robert Hicks and Gayle Jenkins, staged a march from Bogalusa to the Washington Parish Courthouse in Franklinton, about twenty-five miles west of Bogalusa. It was a march staged at night, to highlight the dangers that Blacks risked if they were out after dark in Bogalusa.

The Bogalusa Commission Council had passed a ban against night marches in the city, so the march to Franklinton started at 3:00 p.m. to be sure the marchers would be beyond the city limits before dark. As the marchers made their way to Franklinton overnight, they were accompanied by about fifty state police. They arrived in Franklinton about 9:00 a.m. the next morning and capped the successful procession by singing what had become the civil rights anthem, "We Shall Overcome," at the steps of the parish courthouse.

Only a few days later, A. Z. Young announced another march that would eclipse the Selma marches—at least in terms of distance. The Alabama marches from Selma to the state capital in Montgomery were a little over fifty miles. Young announced on July 28 that a march would begin two weeks later, on August 10, from Bogalusa to the state capital in Baton Rouge—106 miles. At the capitol building, the protesters would present a list of grievances and demands to Governor John McKeithen.

On that date, a Thursday, about twenty-five marchers began their way south from Bogalusa along Louisiana Highway 21 to Covington in St. Tammany Parish. Over the next ten days, the crowd of marchers grew as it headed west along US Highway 190 from Covington through Hammond in Tangipahoa Parish and Denham Springs in Livingston Parish to Baton Rouge in East Baton Rouge Parish. The group bivouacked each night along the way.

The marchers were harassed and attacked even though they were under escort by hundreds of state police and Louisiana National Guardsmen. Along the way, the column of marchers was jeered and spat at— or upon—by KKK supporters. Bottles, rocks, and eggs were thrown at them. Glass was broken in the highway to make the marcher's progress more difficult. When the group approached the eastern edge of Baton Rouge after more than a week of walking, the last night on the road featured competing rallies. As the protesters were celebrating the near-completion of their march at Capital Junior High School, the Ku Klux Klan was counter-rallying in a nearby field.

When the crowd of marchers that had grown to 600, and their local supporters from Baton Rouge, arrived at the state capitol the next day, they were greeted by 300 Klan supporters. The climaxing rally was watched over by nearly 2,000 state troopers and Guardsmen.

Just before the marches from Bogalusa to Franklinton and to Baton Rouge in July and August, journalist Franklynn Peterson was in Bogalusa to do a piece on the Deacons for Defense for the August edition of the Catholic publication *Ave Maria*. He wrote: "With moderate voices silenced, Bogalusa is back to normal: Unless you're on the scene when something happens—controversial or not—you'll never know about it listening to the two remaining radio stations. And the *Bogalusa Daily News* is the most extreme middle-of-the-road publication in the country: it prints separate Negro and White editions."

What do I think of Peterson's characterization of the paper as the "most extreme middle-of-the-road publication in the country"? Well, nothing really. A man's opinion is his own. But I can note that the separate Black edition of the paper that he held up as evidence for his assertion had been ended as soon as I took the publisher's chair a few years earlier. News of Bogalusa's Blacks and whites was being published side-by-side for three years before Peterson hit town.

The marches were one of the highlights of those years of tension, in terms of the national publicity. After those few years of Bogalusa having plenty of publicity—most of it very bad—it seemed that the Ku Klux Klan and its splinter groups were appearing to evaporate. There was an overriding current of moderation after those days. Bogalusa has since then, through the efforts of a small nonvocal group of people, continued to make efforts to further the cause of moderation to bring about overall improvements in the city.

A. Z. Young continued as a leader of the Black community locally and across the state. He later served as executive assistant for minority affairs and in various other positions in the multiple administrations of Governor Edwin Edwards, and upon his death in 1993 he was the first Black Louisianan to lie in state at the Louisiana state capitol. Along the Louisiana Civil Rights Trail, a state historical marker was erected in 2018 to mark his Bogalusa home, and a park in Baton Rouge is named in his memory.

Hicks, a founder of the Deacons for Defense and a leader of the Voters League and the marches, was also a leader of the local civil rights movement in the courts. In federal court, he sued Police Chief Claxton Knight to gain protection of demonstrators by Bogalusa police. He sued the Crown Zellerbach Corporation to end hiring and promotion discrimination in the Bogalusa paper mill and as a result became the first Black supervisor in the mill and held the position until his retirement. He sued the Department of Housing and Urban Development to block construction of a low-rent housing complex in Bogalusa; he said such projects perpetuated segregation. He sued the Bogalusa School Board to fully desegregate the city's schools. He died in 2010 at the age of 81. His home in Bogalusa is also marked by a historical marker as part of the Louisiana Civil Rights Trail and is listed on the National Register of Historic Places.

Bascom Talley, my supporter throughout the challenges of those years earlier and a good friend after that, died in 1971, at age 55. It was too soon. I might not have become publisher without his good words to Milt Wick, and getting through those earlier tough years would have been more difficult—and lonely—without his support and friendship had he gone any sooner.

The perceived aura of moderation was less evident in the rural areas of Washington Parish; it may have been quiet out there and the fire may have been contained, but it was not out. Even in the city, many things had not really changed in the years immediately following the late 1960s. The 1970s and 1980s continued to be marked by obvious racial differences. Most of the problems during those two decades involved the public education system, racial balance, and schoolyard and school hall fights.

In the late 1960s and into the 1970s, after several years of bad publicity, Bogalusa and Washington Parish had some positives to focus on as local Black athletes and others—products of the segregated all-Black schools that were coming to an end—accomplished noteworthy achievements beyond Bogalusa and the parish.

In 1969, Leslie Charles "Charlie" Spikes was the New York Yankees' first-round pick in Major League Baseball's amateur draft, after he had graduated as a star baseball player at Central Memorial. Spikes had some early success in the Yankees organization but was traded and made his mark in "The Bigs" with the Cleveland Indians from 1973 to 1977. Because he was a power hitter, leading the Indians in homeruns for several of his years there, he had been nicknamed "The Bogalusa Bomber."

During his heyday in Cleveland, when he was playing more regularly than later in his career with Atlanta and Detroit, the *Daily News* sports page every day featured "Spikes Spotlight"—a boxed recap of how Bogalusa's professional baseball player had done in the previous night's game. After five years in Cleveland, Spikes played one year for the Detroit Tigers, then two years with the Atlanta Braves, and he finished his career in 1981 with a year playing for the Chunichi Dragons in Japan.

In 2017, Spikes was featured as Washington Parish's top all-time athlete in New Orleans's NOLA.com series on the top all-time athlete in each of Louisiana's sixty-four parishes, the judgment based on which athlete from each parish had risen to the highest level in his chosen sport. While Spikes was finishing his tenure in Cleveland and spending a year in Detroit, his younger brother Carl Spikes played two years in the Chicago Cubs' minor league organization—in 1977 at Geneva, New York, in the New York–Pennsylvania League, and in 1978 at Pompano Beach, Florida, in the Florida State League.

Perry Brooks was a graduate of Wesley Ray High School in Angie in the northeast corner of the parish, played college football at Southern University in Baton Rouge, and in 1976 was drafted by the National Football League's Washington Redskins as a defensive tackle. He was on the team when the Redskins won Super Bowl XVII in January of 1983, defeating the Miami Dolphins 27-17 for Coach Joe Gibbs. That off-season, while home to see his parents, Brooks visited the *Daily News* to do an interview and show off his Super Bowl ring. He died in Woodbridge, Virginia, in 2010 at the age of fifty-five.

Off the field, Joseph "Joe" Dyer—born in Gibson, Louisiana, but a resident of the city from the age of two years—became one of the first Black journalists at a major television station (KNXT, later to become KCBS) in Los Angeles. He had been a star athlete before graduating from the segregated Central Memorial High School in 1953, and after graduating from Grambling State University in 1957, he served four years in the US Air Force.

There, he was editor of the base newspaper at the Grand Forks, North Dakota, Air Force Base, and afterward went to Los Angeles to be an actor. But in 1965 he was hired by KNXT, and almost immediately he provided reporting on the famed Watts Riots that were part of the Civil Rights unrest. Dyer stayed with KNXT-KCBS for the next thirty years, reporting the news, writing and presenting editorials, becoming a top executive at the station, and earning nearly 200 community service awards. He retired in 1995.

During his career he had written both history and fiction, and in 2002, he wrote his memoir, *A Retired Black Television Broadcaster's Lifetime of Memories: From Cotton Fields to CBS*. He died in 2011 at the age of seventy-six.

James William Brown—later to become known as the Pulitzer Prize–winning poet Yusef Komunyakaa—was born in Bogalusa; after high school he joined the US Army in 1969 and served during the Vietnam War. Like Dyer, he worked as a writer and then as editor on a military newspaper, the 23rd Infantry Division's *Southern Cross*. He was awarded a Bronze Star for his service in Vietnam.

After the Army, he attended the University of Colorado and began writing poetry in 1973 for a creative writing class. He earned his bachelor's degree at Colorado, then earned master's degrees subsequently at Colorado State University and the University of California-Irvine, and went on to teach English and creative writing at the University of New Orleans, the University of Indiana, Princeton University, and New York University.

In 1984, his first published book, *Copacetic,* included poems that reflected on his experiences while growing up in segregated Bogalusa. Two years later he published *I Apologize for the Eyes in My Head,* and two years after that came *Dien Cai Dau* about his experiences in Vietnam. In 1994, he was awarded the Pulitzer Prize for Poetry for his newest collection, *Neon Vernacular: New and Selected Poems.* Since then, he has continued to teach and write and has produced numerous additional collections and earned numerous additional awards for his work.

After a decade of criticism by both sides about the way the *Daily News* covered Bogalusa's black-white divide, my decision to not report every school-yard fracas still held. And people still complained.

In 1975, with racial troubles popping up every now and again at the fully integrated high school and junior high campuses, a committee representing the Black community sent a letter to Bogalusa School Board President Emmett Breland and city Commissioner of Safety Carl Jarrel, with copies to School Superintendant Frank Mobley, high school principals J. L. Bickham and Tommy Leos, junior high principal Gary Holcomb, Mayor Louis Rawls, the state Superintendant of Education and the state Attorney General, and federal officials and judges in New Orleans. The letter cited racial incidents, including the stabbing of a Black student by a white student, at the schools on December 3, 4, and 5.

The group asked for a December 8 meeting with the City School Board—even though the letter was dated that same day and not mailed until December 9—to discuss the civil and personal rights of the Black students they said were being violated. The group called for the white student who stabbed the Black to be brought to trial.

They wanted, for all Black students who had been charged by police in any of the fracases, to have their police records be wiped clean and their bonds be voided and refunded, and any who had been expelled or suspended be allowed back at school immediately pending a hearing for reinstatement. They also asked for full reports on incidents of the previous days, and about any "nonprofessional" behavior by teachers, Black or white.

A. Z. Young was the lead signatory on the letter, and ten other members of the committee, which had not given itself a name, also signed.

Then they issued a call to the *Daily News*—I had been copied on the letter.

They wanted "[b]etter journalism techniques and reporting to be applied immediately by the *Bogalusa Daily News* in this matter and future events. If the present practice is continued, this committee will, without hesitation, seek an injunction to cease publication of the *Bogalusa Daily News*."

I was amused that this group of community leaders were naïve enough to think that they could go to court and have the paper shut down, or—if they actually knew in their hearts that that wouldn't happen—that the threat of trying to do so would convince me to suddenly change the way I operated the paper after a dozen years as publisher.

Even after the open flames of white supremacy in the middle 1960s had burned out, for some the embers of longing for a return to the Klan's good old days remained in places across the country, and public Klan activity popped up locally through the years.

In April 1976, a revived local Klan unit—The Invisible Empire Knights of the Ku Klux Klan, Realm of Louisiana Lodge W-27—opened a new headquarters building on Superior Avenue, and their announcement flyer announced there would even be a Klan parade through town to the new (and for the first time, public) location. I don't recall if the parade actually happened, nor how long the headquarters stayed open, but the mayor of the city at the time was the dignitary ribbon cutter for the grand event. Mayor Louis Rawls said it was only fair to do the honors for a new establishment in town. For his services, the mayor was declared an honorary member of the Klan. The story was carried in papers across the country under headlines such as:

KKK Rides Again
(Ada, Oklahoma)

Klan Set to Launch Louisiana Comeback
(Burlington, North Carolina)

New KKK Leaders Feel That Respectability Helps Recruiting
(Pocatello, Idaho)

In 1983, whoever was in what was left of the Klan in Bogalusa at the time held a public rally at the edge of the city. Their poster did not state which group of the Klan was hosting the rally, but the featured speaker, Bill Wilkinson of Denham Springs, near Baton Rouge, had recently been the Imperial Wizard of the Invisible Empire, Ku Klux Klan. "We of the Ku Klux Klan are unapologetically committed to the interests, ideas and cultural values of the White Majority," their announcement flyer declared.

Even at that time, the *Daily News* came under criticism for its coverage of Bogalusa's civil rights activity twenty years earlier. In 1985, one of Lou Jr.'s high school classmates who was then living and teaching in Puerto Rico forwarded to me a letter to the editor clipped from the *San Juan Star.*

Harold J. Lidin, president of the Roman Catholic group Pax Cristi in Puerto Rico, recalled his memory of Bogalusa's troubles, and how he remembered the *Daily News* reporting of them. He referenced the *Daily*

News as he complained about a lack of local news coverage in Puerto Rico, where the storage of nuclear weapons at a US naval base on the island was a controversial topic.

Lidin wrote of Bogalusa in the 1960s: "Dramatic confrontations exploded time and time again; on Bogalusa streets by day, on national television by night. And on the front pages of hundreds of daily newspapers. . . . But not in Bogalusa. What for hundreds of other editors was a mighty drama was for the editors of the Bogalusa newspaper nothing more than a fracas, a minor case of disturbing the peace. And it was played accordingly. Back on page nine or thereabouts."

My thoughts on that? The same as when journalist Franklynn Peterson knocked us in *Ave Maria* in 1967: a man's opinion is his own.

In November 2008, Cynthia Lynch of Oklahoma was murdered at a "Klan" initiation gone bad in a secluded area of neighboring St. Tammany Parish. She had traveled from Tulsa to meet the organizers with whom she had been communicating online. Nine men and women from the Bogalusa area were at Lynch's initiation into the group that called itself the Sons of Dixie Knights of the Ku Klux Klan.

After her arrival and spending a few days with the group, Lynch expressed second thoughts about joining, and died for her doubts. In 2010, Raymond Foster of Bogalusa pleaded guilty to second degree murder and was sentenced to life in prison. At the time of the killing, officials in Washington and St. Tammany Parishes were quick to denounce the group as KKK "wannabees" and declared that the real Klan no longer existed.

Maybe the Klan as we knew it in the 1960s did not really exist by 2008 and, one hopes, does not now.

While integration has now long been a reality at public governmental and quasi-governmental affairs, social segregation among the population is in many places still as distinct in some forms as it was in the 1960s, including in Bogalusa and Washington Parish.

America remembers passage of the Civil Rights and Voting Rights Acts of 1964 and 1965, when the nation's government had to respond to the intolerance and indignity of man against man. But racial divide in the United States has not yet been conquered and hatred still lives.

The Klan's legacy may never end. Though far less common than in the 1960s, pickup trucks bearing a front Confederate flag license plate can still be seen throughout the South. In those horrid Klan days, that license plate was considered to be almost as symbolic of the idea of white supremacy as the KKK's burning cross.

The Ku Klux Klan motto, "Yesterday, Today, Tomorrow, and Forever" will long be remembered by law-abiding citizens who stood up to the Klan and had a part in its demise toward the end of the twentieth century. While some form of the Klan may still exist in some parts of the country, it is for the most part regarded as a throwback to a time when some people were unable or unwilling to accept the responsibilities of human rationality.

It is often said that the only thing that heals hurt is the passage of time. How long will it take, America? A half-century of effort has shown progress, but only in people's hearts can the full measure be accomplished.

AFTERWORD

LOU MAJOR JR.

For more than the first half of his career of fifty-plus years in community journalism, Marion L. "Lou" Major was editor, and then publisher, of the *Bogalusa Daily News*, and after that he was president and CEO of Wick Communications, which owned the *Daily News*. He completed his career, in retirement from active newspapering, as a member of Wick's board of directors. Even as CEO of a news company with nearly thirty papers in eleven states across the country, he worked from an office at the *Daily News*, communicating with the newspapers under his charge by telephone, fax, email, and plane ticket. His entire newspaper career was spent at 525 Avenue V in Bogalusa.

But he did not put his memories to paper until he was completely "out of the business"—until he was no longer going to the *Daily News* office as a reporter, or editor, or publisher, or CEO, or board member. He finished this memoir a year or two before his death from lymphoma in 2012 at age 82. His wife of 63 years, Peggy, my Mom, died in 2014.

Though he was born in 1930 in Meridian, Mississippi, while his father was posted there for a year as a US Postal Service rail car mail clerk, Lou Major grew up in New Orleans and adjacent Jefferson Parish, Louisiana. After graduating from St. Aloysius High School in New Orleans, he spent a year at Tulane University before completing his journalism education at Louisiana State University in Baton Rouge. Right out of LSU, he and Peggy moved to Bogalusa when he joined the staff at the *Bogalusa Daily News* as a cub reporter in June 1951. He worked his way up, was publisher of the paper a dozen years later, and had only held the position as the newspaper's top executive for about a year when, in 1963, he began guiding the newspaper—at the age of 34—through a several-year period that was difficult for the community of Bogalusa and Washington Parish and for the *Daily News.*

Much has been written of the civil rights days of the middle 1960s in Bogalusa. In all of the after-the-fact analysis of that period of the civil rights movement and of Bogalusa's part in that history, very little has been written about the role played by the *Daily News* and its young publisher. Perhaps that is because he did not self-publicize or self-aggrandize. He did not grant many interviews, he rejected speaking invitations, and he did not testify at congressional hearings. He just stayed at his desk and did his job running the paper.

This memoir is not a full recapitulation of everything that occurred during those civil rights days in Bogalusa and Washington Parish. As he noted in his introduction, other writers have done that in far greater detail. Rather, this is Lou Major's recollection of that period that centers, more than anything else, on his and the *Bogalusa Daily News'* stand against the Ku Klux Klan during that period.

I had the privilege of working with my dad at the *Daily News* for nearly all of my own newspaper career. Not many sons get to work with their father for the better part of an adult lifetime, and fewer can say that they treasure it, as I did. But I got to talk newspapering with him at work and then when we were together at home after work or on weekends. For me, it was simply a continuation of growing up and "talking shop" with a talented, respected newsman.

Years after that turbulent time in the 1960s, my dad occasionally acknowledged privately during some of those kitchen-table conversations that some of the decisions he made regarding news coverage of that period—what local events were covered by the *Daily News* and some of the editorials he wrote—would likely have been different had they benefited from the wisdom that additional years of experience publishing a small-town daily newspaper would bring. He might have paid more attention to why Bogalusa's Black residents felt they had to form the

Deacons for Defense. He might have been more understanding about the role that the Congress of Racial Equality (CORE) was playing on the local Blacks' behalf rather than criticizing them in editorials as outside troublemakers.

When he reflected on those years later on, considering how he might have done things differently as *Daily News* publisher, he consistently said that one thing about those days that would not have been different was the *Daily News*'s stance against the KKK. Under his guidance, the newspaper was, if nothing else, the leading voice in the community to publicly stand against the wretchedness that was the Ku Klux Klan.

To fill in the memory gaps to which Dad confessed in his introduction, some details of events of that period have been added. Also added is some historical background about Bogalusa and Washington Parish's history of racial violence, as well as material that helps place what was happening in the city and parish into the broader timeline of civil rights activity across the nation.

But make no mistake: this is very much Lou Major's work. It is *his* story, *his* memories, and *his* thoughts about events that were of great importance in Bogalusa and Washington Parish when he was a young newspaper publisher—events that were more than mere footnotes in the national civil rights story of the 1960s.

Because the *Daily News*'s editorial battle with the Ku Klux Klan was as an organization and not its individual members, the names of the local Klansmen who fought segregation—even by sometimes violent means— are not included in this memoir. The names of the public officials and the leaders of the Black community who were struggling for their God- and law-given rights are included. But the Klansmen, for all their faults, were still loving parents, grandparents, uncles, or dear family friends to many of the people who still live in Bogalusa and Washington Parish. Dad did not intend his memoir to embarrass the living for the deeds of the departed. Those names, for those who want to know them, can be found in other books about that time, in court records, and in the Congressional Record.

The same is true of the Klan supporters who wrote letters to the editor—some of the more civil ones were published in the paper—that challenged the *Daily News*'s stand against the Klan. Others wrote to Dad as the *Daily News* publisher but not for publication, or they wrote to him personally. Those writers never expected that their names on the letters bearing their thoughts at the time would end up in a memoir written more than fifty years later. Their thoughts, though anonymous in this memoir, are insightful enough when coupled with the actions of the civil rights leaders and public officials dealing with the issues at the time.

When he was inducted into the Hall of Fame at Louisiana State University's Manship School of Journalism in 2010, he was being honored for his fifty-year Louisiana-based newspapering career and in no small part for his guidance of the *Daily News* and its stand against the Klan during troubled times nearly five decades earlier. As he accepted the award, he noted the issues he was juggling at the beginning of his publishing career: "Those were trying times, when I had to balance between the safety of my family, the good of the community, the health of the newspaper," and after a beat, ". . . and not getting fired."

While our dad, and also certainly our mom, worried about the family's safety in the face of threats and harassment by the Klan, my younger siblings and I were, for the most part, blissfully ignorant of the stress of the situation at that time. I cannot honestly say that, as a young teenager, I was truly aware of the scope of what was happening in the city. What I remember was the burning crosses and other "gifts" that the Klan left on our front lawn, and I remember enduring some threats, name-calling, and being ostracized by some of my classmates at Bogalusa Junior High School and then at Bogalusa High.

In the first years of full school desegregation that followed, my brother Steven, two years younger, was roughed up a time or two—by white students who were apparently visiting the perceived sins of our father on his son. My sister Christie, a year behind Steven, confided—not to Dad, but years later to her husband—that she felt her dating life in high school had been compromised "by being the daughter of Lou

Major." And our youngest sibling, Jason, was then only about seven or eight years old and says he remembers only "the good times"—the fun of roasting marshmallows on a burning cross or the weirdness of finding a tombstone on our front doorstep or waking to find our lawn covered with outdated rodeo posters.

In the decades following the 1960s, Dad continued to operate the *Daily News* in a fashion that would serve the good of the community. When I posted the announcement of his death on Facebook in 2012, a former Bogalusan who was, like me, a teenager during the times of racial trouble, commented: "A hearty amen to his hard work and reporting the news during Bogalusa's darkest time—the middle Sixties. As I look back, I realize what courage it took to do that job and do it in an ethical and bold fashion." A leading Bogalusa businessman who had known him for many years observed: "He was a very private person, quiet, somewhat of a 'shadow' to the public, yet he was clearly recognized as one of the most influential men in the parish."

Dad occasionally thought aloud many years later—after we kids were all adults—that he had not been as good a father as he might have been, because he did not spend as much time doing "dad" things with us— coaching us in Little League, taking us fishing, building a treehouse, and the like—as many other fathers do, because he spent so much time at the *Daily News*.

But we disabused him of that notion; we cherished our time with him as kids and as adults. And despite the few difficulties that came our way back then as the sons and daughter of Lou Major, we've all felt that we learned from observation of our dad a very important life lesson: that peer pressure, threats, or the need for personal sacrifice should not dissuade one from always trying to "do the right thing."

In this memoir written shortly before his death, Lou Major put to paper his recollections about doing what he thought was "the right thing"—for better or worse and no going back to change it—in that set of circumstances, at that time, in that place.

CPSIA information can be obtained
at www.ICGtesting.com
Printed in the USA
LVHW091407090221
678821LV00017B/55/J